D0466877

Benchmarking

Benchmarking

A Signpost to Excellence in Quality and Productivity

BENGT KARLÖF
and
SVANTE ÖSTBLOM

Translated by Alan J. Gilderson

JOHN WILEY & SONS
Chichester · New York · Brisbane · Toronto · Singapore

Original Swedish version published under the title of *Bench Marking:*
Vägvisare till mästerskap i produktivitet och kvalitet by Svenska Dagbladets
Förlags AB

Copyright © 1993 by Bengt Karlöf and Svante Östblom

English translation © 1993 by Bengt Karlöf and Svante Östblom

English translation published 1993 by John Wiley & Sons Ltd,
          Baffins Lane, Chichester,
          West Sussex PO19 1UD, England

Reprinted May 1994, March 1995

All rights reserved.

No part of this book may be reproduced by any means,
or transmitted, or translated into a machine language
without the written permission of the publisher.

Other Wiley Editorial Offices

John Wiley & Sons, Inc., 605 Third Avenue,
New York, NY 10158–0012, USA

Jacaranda Wiley Ltd, 33 Park Road, Milton,
Queensland 4064, Australia

John Wiley & Sons (Canada) Ltd, 22 Worcester Road,
Rexdale, Ontario M9W 1L1, Canada

John Wiley & Sons (SEA) Pte Ltd, 37 Jalan Pemimpin #05-04,
Block B, Union Industrial Building, Singapore 2057

Library of Congress Cataloging-in-Publication Data

Karlöf, Bengt, *1939–*
 [Bench marking. English]
 Benchmarking : a signpost to excellence in quality and
productivity / Bengt Karlöf and Svante Östblom; translated
by Alan J. Gilderson.
  p. cm.
 Includes bibliographical references and index.
 ISBN 0-471-94180-8 (cloth)
 1. Benchmarking (Management) I. Östblom, Svante. II. Title.
HD62.15.K3713 1993
658.5'62 – dc20   93–5131
                  CIP

British Library Cataloguing in Publication Data

A catalogue record for this book is available from the British Library

ISBN 0-471-94180-8

Typeset in 11/13 pt Palatino from author's disks by
Dobbie Typesetting Ltd, Tavistock, Devon
Printed and bound in Great Britain by Biddles Ltd, Guildford and King's Lynn

Contents

Preface

Benchmarking is a continuous, systematic process for comparing your own efficiency in terms of productivity, quality and practices with those companies and organizations that represent excellence.

Management buzzwords come and go. Their semantic clarity is often unsatisfactory, and the efficacy of models, methods and approaches varies within wide limits. It is undoubtedly true that waves of fashion roll over the somewhat fuzzily defined field of management. Concepts such as internal marketing, time compression and endless variations on the theme of quality are launched and highlighted from time to time, not infrequently at the instigation of us consultants.

Sometimes these models and approaches look like "rain-dances" performed by the parts of an organization whose function is to promote change and activity in general. Many activities are started without any particular purpose other than to demonstrate that something progressive is being done.

At first sight, benchmarking may appear to be just the latest fashion in management. But benchmarking is not a management fad; it possesses an unusually large content of substance. Let us, without anticipating our introductory chapter, consider some of the factors that explain why this is so.

Large areas of our organized world exist in conditions of planned economy. Departments of companies make internal deliveries to users who in practice are not free to choose alternative suppliers. Although the result of a company at the aggregate level can be read from its accounts, there are many functional parts of it which are not subject to measurement of performance in terms of profit and loss. Benchmarking offers a substitute for the spur to efficiency that is one of the functions of a free market economy. When the unseen hand of market forces is not there to compel efficiency (the function of value and productivity), benchmarking performs that function instead. The same thing applies to all tax-financed systems, which likewise lack the spur to efficiency of a free market economy.

Apart from its effect of closing gaps in productivity or quality, the effect of benchmarking on the development of organizations has astonished us. We call this phenomenon benchlearning. The process of making people adopt the practices of their benchmarking partners removes any blinkers they may be wearing and opens their minds; it creates a learning organization in the true sense of the term. Without being ecstatic about it, we can justifiably claim that this makes the personnel manager's dream come true—the dream of integrating education, leadership development and organizational dynamics with the actual work being done, and of making that work more efficient in terms of quality and productivity.

Benchmarking, as we see it, thus exerts a powerful leverage effect on the organization. Its force for survival would therefore seem to be beyond doubt, as we hope to prove in this book.

We welcome counsel and comments on the contents from readers.

1
Introduction

When somebody writes a book about an idea, readers are apt to get the impression that the authors regard the idea they are describing as the only road to salvation. Such is not the case here. Both of us work for a consultancy firm that uses a variety of models and approaches to develop organizations and companies. We do not believe that any particular doctrine is the sole path to salvation, but that leaders in business and administration must choose the tools, approaches and models best suited to themselves and their circumstances.

There are plenty of advocates of a single method, whether it be called PIMS, TRIM, LOTS, Lean Production or something else. Consultants can get away with this kind of one-track behaviour as long as the market, i.e. management, is relatively ignorant of the available options. Over the past decade, however, we have noted a substantial increase in awareness of methods and approaches among business people. Knowledge of the art of management as such, which is neither economics, engineering nor law, has grown much more widespread. However, much still remains to be done.

Having said that, we must hasten to add that we have yet to work with a method that offers so much inherent potential for improvement as benchmarking. There are many reasons for this, but on a relatively high level of abstraction we can cite two:

1 Benchmarking is aimed directly at increasing operative and strategic efficiency, i.e. the actual content of an organization's work.

2 This leads to a reorientation of culture towards learning, skill enhancement and efficiency, which in turn leads to an unsurpassed process of development.

Benchmarking, properly applied, is an incomparably effective means of improving the organization that uses it. Over the past few years we have been involved with numerous organizations of varying size. We have approached the theory behind the concept of benchmarking by the route of solid practical experience with several organizations, and we have seen the powerful influence that benchmarking exerts on their behaviour, values, methods and aims.

Fairly recent studies of competitiveness in business have underlined the power of a well-run benchmarking process. The MIT Commission on Industrial Productivity found, for example, that a common characteristic of the best-performing companies in North America, regardless of size, is that they apply benchmarking to their products, functions and practices, using the leading companies in their respective fields as references. Similarly, effective application of external benchmarking is one of the criteria for the coveted Malcolm Baldrige National Quality Award.

The situation is the same in Europe; the Swedish Institute for Quality Development, for example, emphasizes "Learn from Others" in its guidelines, and is launching a powerful drive to promote benchmarking in 1993.

In the first two chapters of this book we shall have more to say about the two aspects that make benchmarking such an effective tool for accomplishing change. In the remaining chapters we describe the method stage by stage, giving practical examples designed to help the reader to apply it in various situations.

EFFICIENCY: DEFINITION AND DYNAMICS

When we started working on this book, we naturally read up on the existing literature on benchmarking and related subjects such as quality and productivity. Nowhere did we find that any author had tried to go back and look for the fundamental explanation of why benchmarking has proved so successful.

In most cases benchmarking is treated simply as an approach, which of course it is. It may however be helpful to readers if we go back and try to understand what makes this method so powerful.

The superiority of a free market economy compared to a planned economy actually depends on one thing only: the fact that the customer is always free to choose between alternative suppliers. However, no such freedom exists in the great majority of economic activities, whether in the public sector or in business. We refer here to all those departments of companies and organizations which deliver to other departments of the same organizations. Recipients of goods and services in such macrosystems hardly ever have any real freedom to choose their suppliers.

We can thus note that although a company can measure its aggregate efficiency from its profit-and-loss account, the aggregate conceals much undefined room for improvement within individual subfunctions. The value of benchmarking is that it provides a substitute for the efficiency-boosting effect of market forces in units that are not exposed to market economics. Pressure to be efficient diminishes with distance from the customer.

The purpose of all organized activity is

TO CREATE VALUE WHICH IS GREATER THAN THE COST OF CREATING IT.

This statement, in all its platitudinous simplicity, embodies the profound truth that is the driving force of all economic activity, and embraces all the components that the management of an organization can influence. It applies to *all* organized activity, not just economic activity. The value concerned can be of many kinds. Churches, co-operatives, professional associations and trade unions, for example, must offer something of value to their members which the members regard as higher than the cost of their membership dues. The same criterion applies to time, effort or anything else expended for the sake of getting something worth while. The public sector is currently experiencing a crisis in so far as many of its operations fail, in the opinion of many people, to contribute anything of value to the common weal. We shall have more to say about this later.

The special advantage of the benchmarking method is that it provides an incentive for non-competitive parts of the staff organizations that manage companies to improve their efficiency. Let us therefore review the various components of efficiency.

Efficiency

The concept of efficiency is made up of four basic components:

1 Quality (utility).
2 Price.
3 Production volume.
4 Cost.

Value is the quotient of quality and price. It is value that determines how many units are sold in a free market economy, i.e. one where the customer has a free choice of what to buy.

The quotient of production volume and cost is called productivity. The motive force for efficiency in a market economy, then, is that the value which is delivered, and which the customer is willing to pay for, must be higher than the cost of producing a unit of the product or service that represents the value.

Thus efficiency is a function of value and productivity. The graph in Figure 1 illustrates the relationship. The cost per unit produced should logically determine the lowest price that can be charged, if the producing company is to stay in business in the long term. Quality or utility, on the other hand, should determine the highest price that customers are willing to pay.

So while the unit cost of production is important with regard to the price that must be charged in the long term, the customer's perception of quality is decisive with regard to the acceptable cost of production because it sets the maximum price. Modern management has begun to apply "reverse engineering" to a growing extent. This proceeds from the customer's perception of value, meaning quality in relation to price, and works back from there to decide the acceptable cost of producing goods or services.

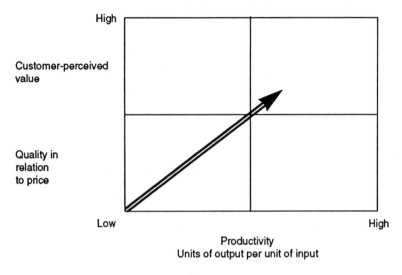

EFFICIENCY MATRIX

Figure 1

Let us take a few examples to illustrate the relationships expressed in the Figure 1 graph and definitions. We thus find that inefficiency, in principle, can imply one of two things.

In the first case the value delivered may be acceptable to the market, but the operation is inefficient because the cost of producing the value is greater than the price paid for it. Two current examples of this situation are Saab and Jaguar cars. A given Saab or Jaguar model fetches a given market price which customers are willing to pay for the value that a Saab or Jaguar represents to its owner. The problem is that both factories are inefficient today because the costs of developing, manufacturing and distributing their cars are higher than the prices that the market is willing to pay. The reason for their inefficiency is that productivity is too low.

Let us stay with the analogy of the automotive industry to illustrate the second case. Let us imagine that the evil-smelling little East German Trabant could be manufactured with Japanese productivity, less than 30 man-hours per vehicle. Even if this were possible, there would still be no future in manufacturing Trabants because their quality in relation to price—any price— would still not persuade customers to buy them. That, incidentally, is one of the major problems of the former Eastern Bloc. The goods sold in the shops of Moscow, Prague and St Petersburg are quite unsaleable in Western Europe with the quality standards that customers have come to expect there. Price ceases to exist as the denominator in a quotient of value where the quality is so poor that price no longer makes any difference.

One of the gigantic problems in the welfare economies of Western Europe is the existence of numerous large systems which, however productive they may be, contribute too little of value to society. Our public sectors abound with luxury production whose value is low but which continues because the customer never has to weigh its quality or utility against the sacrifice he must make to buy it. Let us cite here an example from Sweden, both sublime and ridiculous, of the kind of luxury public production that we all consume:

Almond buns investigated
The Municipal Environment Administration in Stockholm decided that a checkup on almond buns was called for; the almond paste they contained might not always be almond paste. Operation Almond Paste was therefore mounted. Buns were purchased at 52 shops. The investigators found that some of them contained substitutes; but on the other hand the suppliers had not claimed that they were selling the genuine article.

The Environment Administration is in the midst of an economy drive. But morale is important in times of cutbacks, say leading officials, and a bun probe gives the staff something to bite on.
From *Dagens Nyheter*, 14 October 1992

Exactly the same phenomenon exists in all large organizations, whether they be companies, trade unions or something else. Big corporations contain many people and departments who justify their jobs, and their existence, by high productivity—by pressure of supply. People work hard and keep themselves fully occupied making studies and writing reports which are then distributed to recipients within the system. Many staff units justify their existence in this way, by push of supply rather than pull of demand.

The same applies to numerous absurdities that we can observe in the public sectors of various countries in Western Europe. These units actually operate under the conditions of a planned economy. They have substituted internal transactions for market transactions and are thus shielded from the pressure for efficiency that is exerted in a free market economy by the customer's freedom of choice between alternative suppliers.

A planned economy can in fact be characterized as a system which is incapable of producing even that which people do not want.

A planned-economy relationship with the outside world leads in the long term to deteriorating value production and quality as well as lower productivity. One reason why benchmarking has proved to be such a powerful way of making companies more efficient is that it supplies the same lessons and incentives which come from market transactions in a free economy. Benchmarking can be applied to both axes of the value graph, replacing the action of the "invisible hand" in constantly guiding productivity and quality towards improvement.

Efficiency and productivity are too often confused with each other in European debate. Yet the distinction is of monumental importance and needs to be understood by everybody operating in our microeconomies. Classical economics deals mainly with commodity goods, i.e. those whose quality relationships with each other are fully comparable. Such is hardly ever the case in real-life economics. Quality has acquired great importance at a time when that classic unit of economics, the bushel of wheat, has been relegated to a secondary economic role. A car cannot be directly compared with any other car. A Trabant and a Rolls-Royce are not the same thing—a fact which has brought quality into focus in a way which classic economics ignores.

The *raison d'être* of products, departments, administrations and whole companies is called in question today more often and more repeatedly than ever before. The woods are full of competitors and substitutes. If for example you consider the airline business in isolation, ignoring the threat of video conferences as a substitute for its function, your analysis is likely to lead to the wrong conclusions.

Benchmarking, the making of measurements with reference to a fixed datum point, has come into use as the name of a method for measuring and evaluating those parts of an organization which operate under planned-economy conditions. This includes all departments of companies and organizations, as well as practices, productivity figures and quality or customer-perceived value.

The two axes of the efficiency graph and their derivatives are in fact the parameters that a leader can manipulate. All employees, all subcontractors, consultants and owners, must likewise proceed from these parameters to attain short-term or long-term success.

Value, Productivity and People

One of the most difficult dichotomies of businessmanship is the one between productivity, maximized output, on the one hand and value creation, high customer-perceived quality, on the other. We shall discuss this in more detail in the next chapter.

During the eighties, moreover, the realization grew that ability to manage people in an organization in an effective way can help to enhance both customer-perceived quality and the productivity of the organization. This is because of the simple fact that people who are well treated, and therefore feel motivated, make a greater effort to serve the customers who ultimately pay their salaries and wages, and also put much more energy into their work. This leads in turn to a win–win situation in which the employer enjoys increased productivity while at the same time the employees are more content with their lot.

Productivity

Frederick Winslow Taylor was a pioneer in the field of productivity. He was actually the first to apply benchmarking to the case of workers shovelling coal at Bethlehem Steel's steelworks. Taylor's method was simply to identify the best way of performing a given operation and then apply that method to other similar operations.

The pursuit of pure productivity which prevailed from the end of the nineteenth century up to the outbreak of World War II led to ruthless exploitation of labour. During that period the market was at the mercy of capitalists, as it now is in Eastern Europe. The capitalists there have a monopoly, a duopoly or at best an oligopoly with fixed prices and so on. In such a situation customers lack any real freedom of choice, and employers can pursue tough labour productivity policies without restraint. If the workforce likewise lacks acceptable and attractive alternatives, the result tends to be a unilateral, mechanistic focus on labour productivity with a view to maximizing output per man-hour, with no thought given to innovating, improving products or replacing labour with capital.

The notion that people are basically lazy and work-shy, and need to be made by various means to work harder and be more productive, is associated with the name of F. W. Taylor. What neither he nor Karl Marx nor Friedrich Engels foresaw was that capitalism would be drawn into a situation where capitalists would be at the mercy of the market. The hard, mechanistic and callous aspects of capitalism and productivity would then give way to a higher degree of competition, with people as an important competitive factor. When people are motivated to serve customers better and enjoy their work in an ever more knowledge-oriented world with fewer monotonous production-line jobs, the very keystone of Marxism falls and the great issue of the twentieth century is resolved. This is one important reason why the world is growing more performance-oriented. For an organization to succeed—and feel successful—in an environment of more players and harder competition, all parts of the system must be exposed to competition so that they can improve their performance. The various stages in the potential improvement of productivity are well described in the Experience Curve. This was first formulated by the commanding officer of the Wright–Patterson Air Force Base, the US Government's aviation research centre, in 1926. He discovered that for every time the accumulated production of a component doubled, the unit cost fell by 20–30 per cent. The reason was not that a large fixed cost was distributed among more units, but learning, practice and changes in the work organization. The underlying factors of the Experience Curve are listed below:

Factors in the Experience Curve
1 Labour productivity, practice.
2 Work organization; specialization and structure.
3 Production process; inventions and improvements.
4 Balance between labour and capital; value added per employee.

5 Product standardization; balance between stability and innovation.
6 Technical specialization; cheaper production with specialized equipment.
7 Redesign; value analysis to economize on materials, energy and labour.
8 Economies of scale (see below).

The reader who is interested in productivity and benchmarking in the context of productivity should note that economies of scale are something distinct from the effects of the Experience Curve. The former are the result of fixed costs being distributed among a large number of manufactured units, whereas the latter are a combination of advantages achieved through repetition, specialization, rationalization, replacement of labour by capital, and so on.

Value

The concept of value likewise has a relatively short history viewed on a long time scale. Just as the notion of productivity can be attributed to F.W. Taylor, so can that of value creation be attributed to Heinrich Gossen. It was he who solved the riddle that economists from Adam Smith onward had puzzled over. Attempts had long been made to derive the value of a product from the labour that went into its production. Even the brilliant Adam Smith, the father of economic science, had failed to explain the meaning of value.

Heinrich Gossen, an otherwise undistinguished Austrian economist, cracked the problem in the mid-nineteenth century. The riddle can be epitomized and simplified by the following question:

Why is a glass of water so useful but worth so little, while a bag of diamonds is so useless but worth so much?

This question can hardly be answered in terms of labour input. Gossen's contribution to the solution lay in the following intriguing counter-question:

If you were dying of thirst in the middle of the Sahara, would you not be willing to trade a sizeable quantity of diamonds for a litre of water?

Thus was formulated what is known as the Theory of Marginal Utility, which is formulated as follows:

The marginal utility of an article is the addition to total utility or satisfaction generated by the most recently acquired specimen of that article.

A couple of corollaries can be derived from this theory:

1st corollary
The law of diminishing marginal utility implies that the marginal utility of an article to the consumer is inversely proportional to the amount consumed.

2nd corollary
The consumer maximizes total utility by selecting purchases of goods in such a way that the marginal utility of each purchase is equal to that of the purchase of some other article.

We can illustrate this with the following quotation from the Swedish economist Göran Albinsson-Bruhner:

> "If the needs of citizens can be better satisfied by less sausage and more fruit on the breakfast-table, their grocery shopping habits will change accordingly. The rational household constantly strives towards an (ideal but unattainable) optimum condition which is achieved when it is no longer possible to improve matters by transferring a sum of money from one item on the shopping list to another.
> "No corresponding trade-offs are made in public sector budgets. Lump sums are allocated to various central and local government bodies. It would be sheer coincidence if a marginal million contributed equally to the welfare of citizens whether given to the Civil Aviation Authority, a regional hospital or a municipal department of roads."

As we have pointed out above, the basic theory of value is of crucial importance to both social development and commercial enterprise. In a recent conversation with a prominent economist who had studied the subject of productivity in depth, he frankly declared that economists were more interested in learning about macroeconomics than microeconomics. As a result, generally speaking, economists were far too prone to overlook the values generated by various actions, institutions and costs. Although techniques such as cost-benefit analysis and value analysis have existed for a long time, students of national economy have not learned how to weigh utility and quality against price and order their priorities accordingly.

Among companies and organizations it does not seem to be an accepted and recognized aspect of corporate leadership to have mastered the market side of business management in terms of creating value for customers and cultivating demand based on value. In many organizations with which we have had the privilege of working, the benchmarking technique is generally accepted as applicable to costs, productivity, time and practices. However, it is not nearly so well accepted in relation to matters such as quality or value creation. As the observant reader will have gathered, we are keen to strike a blow on behalf of value creation for customers, to get this aspect more generally recognized as a task of management.

It is the duty of a leader to exercise operative skills to generate short-term profitability, as well as strategic skills to secure long-term success. The distinction between operations and strategy is not always clearly made. Even short-term issues may be of strategic importance if they are broad enough to prompt speedy reappraisals. In Figure 2 we have listed the commonest terms used with reference to strategic and operative efficiency.

PERFORMANCE ORIENTATION AND BENCHMARKING

For thousands of years, man has reckoned success in terms of the exercise of power by conquering somebody else's territory to gain possession of its man-made treasures and natural

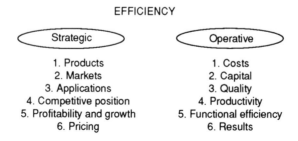

Figure 2

resources. In many large corporations this has long been the prevailing method of growing and showing the outside world that they are successful.

Even during World War II, on the macro-level, this was still the recognized way for nations and rulers to count success. Adolf Hitler's ambition was to grab land in the east and enslave the local populations so that he could secure access to Black Sea oil and arable land, and acquire *Lebensraum*.

The situation was much the same in Hirohito's Japan. The conquest of Manchuria and expansion in the rest of Southeast Asia before and during World War II were prompted by a desire to control natural resources and to win space and success for the Japanese race.

In both cases the strategy of conquest failed, just as it often does in large corporations that seek success solely through structural moves like takeovers and mergers. The two nations concerned have since, through innovation as well as imitation, demonstrated an impressive ability to grow organically. Japan, especially, has been at pains to learn from others in order to build a succession of new platforms for successful behaviour. The process of absorbing many elements of knowledge improves the conditions for creative work.

Benchmarking is the perfect way to seek and attain success through organic growth, i.e. growth based on your own performance. The recent histories of Japan and Germany are excellent examples of how striving for performance-oriented organic growth is a long-term strategy superior to that of conquest by armed might or financial clout.

The Japanese, in particular, have scored outstanding successes since World War II by studying other nations' products, processes and quality standards, and then out-performing them. The comparison between Japan and Russia is highly illustrative. Japan is almost totally devoid of natural resources. All it has are fisheries and a few forests. Yet despite its lack of natural resources, Japan has attained the highest standard of living of any industrialized country in the world.

Russia, by contrast, is loaded with natural resources: oil, diamonds, gold, uranium, forests and arable land. You name it, they have it. Yet Russia today is in a state where it cannot feed its own population, even on the root vegetable level. If a shipment of turnips arrives in Kheraboksi or Chelabinsk, queues form outside the shops.

The former West Germany was likewise one of the world's most successful nations. By concentrating on organic growth and the creation of a national dynamic, the Germans have attained comparable successes—in contrast to the tragedy of World War II, which led only to death and destruction.

It is a well documented fact that leaders of large corporations are power-oriented to a higher degree than the leaders of small and medium-sized companies, and therefore more inclined to put their own personal success before the good of the business. Their method of achieving personal success is often to make spectacular coups in the form of growth by acquisition, divestments, and so forth—in short by portfolio manipulation and corporate structural engineering.

Performance-oriented environments, on the other hand, exhibit less spectacular behaviour consisting of continual striving for improvement of productivity, value creation, capital structure and motivation of the organization and its members. Here benchmarking has proved to be a superior technique for reorienting an organization towards performance.

Performance-oriented people are those who put the good of the business first and measure their own personal success by that yardstick. Let us now proceed to consider some aspects of organization dynamics which have proved to be exceptionally powerful.

Benchmarking and Culture Change

Many discoveries of an intellectual nature seem so simple in hindsight. We must however admit that the power and effect of benchmarking on organization dynamics astonished us. The consequences of benchmarking to organizations can be summed up in two points:

1 Benchmarking focusses attention and energy on work content and performance, thereby initiating a process of learning.
2 Traditional leadership development and training programmes can be integrated with the work content.

Let us then sort the organization development aspects into these two piles and deal with them separately.

Sociologists have long since identified various kinds of social motive systems. Many classifications have been made, but one that has been found applicable in an organizational context is the one devised by David MacLelland. He divides the system of social motives into three categories:

1 Power orientation.
2 Relation orientation.
3 Performance orientation.

Power orientation is manifested in a desire to be at the centre of things, to exercise influence through rewards and repression, and to control one's surroundings. We can also to some extent trace people's choice of careers back to their social motive structures. Power-oriented people are more apt to choose careers that offer opportunities for exercising power. All kinds of authorities fall into this category. Studies have also shown that monopolistic organizations and large corporations are more likely than other organizations to attract power-oriented recruits.

Conversely, the environment influences the people in it. We are all influenced by our environment. This means that organizations which encourage a certain type of behaviour tend to make their individual members act in a power-oriented way: in short, to put their own advancement and the success of their own department before the good of the business and the organization as a whole.

Relation orientation means being motivated by the desire to:

• have good relations with those around them,
• be liked,
• comply unselfishly with others' wishes.

Relation orientation has become much more widespread in the past few decades, encouraged by the expansion of the public sector. Many occupational categories have arisen whose tasks have to do with relations in one form or another. Work in the social services and the service industries has a strong element of relation orientation. The service-providing functions of the public sector have grown enormously compared to the supervisory and operative functions.

Performance orientation is reflected in behaviour that aims at:

- being best,
- getting results,
- winning success through efficiency.

The whole world today is moving in the direction of performance orientation. The greatest issue of our century has been the contest between planned economy and communism on the one hand, and free market economy and capitalism on the other. A well-known historian recently said that steps in human progress hardly ever fall neatly into calendar decades or centuries as we often suppose. In fact, he claims, the nineteenth century did not really end until the outbreak of World War I in 1914. The twentieth century, on the other hand, ended in 1990 with the fall of the Berlin Wall and the collapse of the communist terror regimes in Eastern Europe. The market economy, so to speak, won by a walkover when its opponent keeled over from sheer exhaustion and gave up. Efficiency, defined as value in relation to productivity, has become the decisive factor in promoting a sense of success. The *raisons d'être* of various kinds of organized activity are being called in question, and the value of what is produced is being measured against cost in a manner characteristic of free market economies. This applies particularly to public-sector systems in Western Europe.

This also implies that all institutionalized phenomena are likely to be subjected to ever harder scrutiny from the standpoint of efficiency, i.e. they will be required to justify their continued existence by delivering value in relation to productivity.

This is the prime motive force of business enterprise. Financial operations and portfolio manipulations are of course important subfunctions of enterprise in that they can set up the right structural conditions for success, but they can never achieve success by themselves without sustained performance-oriented behaviour. Japan and Germany are not the only examples. In the corporate world we can see General Motors and many other examples of the failure of power-oriented behaviour to gain long-term success. GM under Ross Perot in the eighties took over both Hughes Aerospace and EDS, but lost market share in its core businesses, cars and goods vehicles.

Now, at the end of 1992, we can see the results. Chairman John Smale, formerly head of Procter & Gamble, has replaced the top management and started a revolution in the power-oriented GM palace.

Power-oriented leadership is no substitute for performance-oriented leadership in the long term. The big European corporations that have tried to grow structurally rather than organically, and in so doing have lost sight of the factors that lead to sustained success, have not done so well in the long term. Benchmarking is an unsurpassed method of directing energy and intelligence towards the most essential thing of all, the content of the work.

This is not to belittle the importance of structural changes, which are sometimes necessary. But we firmly believe that structural operations can only do harm if they are undertaken for the sake of personal aggrandizement rather than for the good of the business. The distinction is by no means clear, but our readers ought to be diagnostically aware of the difference between these two archetypes of growth. Benchmarking, then, is the method that makes the organization focus on organic growth, i.e. on successful competition for the favour of customers, which is the real task of the organization. Structural growth, when it takes place, is generally instigated by top management and does not affect the organization until all the structural operations have been decided on and the transactions made.

Benchmarking and Leadership Development

The aims of traditional leadership are still heavily influenced by a number of articles of faith.

Corporate managements are often indifferent to leadership development, regarding it as a necessary evil. Heads of training departments often lack the status they need to be taken really seriously, and are often excluded from knowledge of the company's aims and plans. As a result, leadership development is often misdirected.

There are a number of reasons for this:

1 Many companies regard leadership development as an act of faith, something which is desirable but which cannot be translated into greater efficiency or higher profits—a non-essential cost.
2 The benefits of leadership development have seldom been demonstrated. The low status of the training staff limits their ability to give truly professional training, and few companies evaluate the results. It is therefore difficult to prove the value of leadership development, which thus becomes little more than a management ritual.
3 Few companies or organizations know the real cost of leadership development. The accounting department keeps a close eye on expenditure on hotels, lecturers, etc., but seldom pays any attention to the salary costs of the participants.
4 There is a clear tendency to run leadership development programmes with a behavioural science bias; this often reflects the training and inclinations of the organizers. As a result, these programmes seldom reflect the real needs of the organization.
5 Leadership development tends in many cases to proceed from the needs of the individual rather than those of the management. The programmes usually comprise elements of individual psychology and group dynamics with no solid foundation in the operations of the business.

There is a great need to get away from the idea that the primary function of leadership development is to improve the individual, to the indirect benefit of the company, and to establish that leadership development is primarily for the sake of the company, while incidentally developing the individual. This shift of emphasis is more than just a play on words.

As long as top management fails to understand and accept the value of leadership development, it will remain the "Cinderella of the organization" (David Hussey). One of the chief functions of leadership development is to relate to the goals and strategies of the organization. There are many who say this, but few who do anything to make it happen. Scandinavian Airlines, for example, should have included rationalization skills in its leadership development programmes in the mid-eighties, but did not do so despite repeated urging from various quarters.

A number of well-known phenomena in management can be viewed as a continuous spectrum. Four major parts of this spectrum are strategy formulation, strategy implementation, leadership development and training programmes. It is an art to achieve consistency in this array of important instruments in the context of a process of change.

When an organization makes a change of course, i.e. when a new strategy is implemented, we find that the actual process of implementation tends to be obstructed by the following factors, in the order given:

1 It took longer than expected.
2 Unforeseen problems arose.
3 The activities were not efficiently co-ordinated.
4 Management did not give its full attention to the matter.
5 The people involved lacked the required skills.
6 Individuals on all levels were insufficiently developed.

Since these are empirically established problems attendant upon organization development and strategy implementation, there ought to be methods of dealing with them. Our experience is that benchmarking is a splendid instrument for the purpose, not just for providing the analytical input for a choice of strategic course, but also for finding ways to improve the content of operations in various respects in a repetitive process combined with effective action.

The conclusion from the above is, then, that benchmarking has a remarkable effect at all stages of the sequence of strategy determination, strategy formulation, strategy implementation, leadership development, organization development and training. At all these stages, the benchmarking method has a unique ability to promote concentration on the task in hand and thus to encourage performance orientation, goal orientation and a drive to get results.

Even well-managed businesses with a good track record on the aggregate level have concealed inefficiencies in various parts of their organization. This applies to horizontal functions as well as vertical processes. Benchmarking is a valuable aid to both detection and correction of such inefficiencies. Let us now link benchmarking to two very important concepts, leadership and businessmanship.

Businessmanship–Leadership–Benchmarking

The definitions of the terms in this heading are vague, and there are moreover special dichotomies that need to be borne in mind in connection with benchmarking.

The term *leadership* normally refers only to the ability to inspire enthusiasm in people and persuade the organization to move in the desired direction. The definition seldom includes strategic ability, i.e. the ability to define a direction for the organization that will be good for all concerned in the long term. Studies made by our firm, Karlöf & Partners, show that an overwhelming majority of active leaders do not include either operative skill or strategic ability in their definition of leadership. By *operative skill* we mean the ability to achieve good results and ensure the short-term success of the organization; this requires precision in dealing with the market and the ability to cope with short-term and long-term problems of productivity.

Strategic ability, on the other hand, refers to the choice of products, markets, investment structures, methods of developing skills, and so on with a view to assuring long-term success and profitability. Not all organizations measure their success in terms of profitability, but in the long run it is always a matter of creating a value which is greater than the cost of producing it.

Businessmanship comprises a number of partly contradictory elements. Briefly, we can define businessmanship as follows:

A businessman is a person who can combine creation of value for customers with economical management of resources in the form of costs and capital. Having an awareness of needs, the businessman can create a value for customers which exceeds the value of the resources consumed and thus generate a profit. He must also have the energy to push issues of development; this is what distinguishes the businessman from the administrator.

One of the advantages of benchmarking is that it focusses people's energy on matters that are essential to the development of their business. Even though we cannot expect all the people in an organization to be businessmen, this focus considerably heightens the business sense of the organization as a whole. Benchmarking, properly applied, creates awareness of both productivity and quality, two of the important elements of businessmanship. In fact the two axes of the efficiency graph with its four components symbolize the essence of business-manship. Let us briefly list some of the dichotomies which characterize the businessman:

Resources—Value
Short-term—Long-term
Leadership—Strategy
Relation—Transaction
People—Activity
Stability—Change

We have already dealt with the first aspect, which concerns creation of value in relation to management of resources. Let us just note, however, that these are two skills which are seldom found together in a single individual. Either we have an aptitude for empathizing with customers' needs and satisfying them, and have little patience with quantification and cost accounting, or else we demand firm structures and computable quantities to work with and deplore the irresponsibility and lack of discipline of salespeople and their ilk. The combination can thus by no means be taken for granted, which explains the dearth of businessmen.

The ability to combine short-term and long-term thinking cannot be taken for granted either. People seldom devote the same amount of energy to the things that need to be done to ensure long-term success as they do to the problems immediately at hand. Short-sightedness, in fact, is one of the besetting sins of business management. Managers put off doing things today which they know will lead to success in the future because it involves too much bother and extra work. A leader who is also a businessman must be capable of both short-term and long-term action.

We have previously mentioned the dichotomy between leadership and strategy. The ability to lead people is actually the opposite of entrepreneurship and high performance motivation. Strongly performance-oriented individuals are generally too lacking in social integration and patience to be good leaders of men.

Most people have never applied businessmanship in practice, but only heard the term mentioned. In our experience, understanding of the term is particularly fuzzy in public-sector organizations which are supposed to be in process of developing a more businesslike orientation.

If you ask a number of people at random what the word businessmanship means to them, they will often associate it with an element of sharp practice, of trying to get the maximum advantage at the other fellow's expense. Many people do not know the difference between a business transaction and a business relationship. Most people have sold a house, a bicycle or a car, and know that the aim in such situations is to try to maximize their own short-term profit.

A business relationship, on the other hand, is an ongoing process that requires two satisfied parties who are willing to go on doing business with each other for a long time. In our experience, repeat business is one of the most underrated criteria of success in business. You can always sell somebody a product or service *once*, and thereby succeed in making a transaction. But you do not know whether you have succeeded in establishing a business relationship until the customer, satisfied with what you have delivered, comes back of his own accord and wants to buy from you again.

We recently read an article written by a famous management guru. His argument was that the companies of today and tomorrow must constantly change their ways—hardly an original thought. One must however bear in mind that constant change stands in direct dichotomy to a high return on investment. If you do not manufacture a given model of car in sufficient numbers, it will never pay back enough to write off your development costs, investments in production, and so on. But on the other hand, if you do as Henry Ford did in the twenties and commit yourself totally to building black Model T Fords, you are headed for disaster. Ford had to shut down his plant in Dearborn, Michigan, for nearly a year to rebuild it. So we cannot pin our hopes on constant change as the key to success, but must strike an optimum balance between stability and change. The thing to do, rather, is to be constantly prepared for change.

Now let us consider benchmarking in relation to the dichotomies we have listed. The method can be used for creation of value and quality as well as for resource management and productivity. It can be applied to relatively trivial short-term problems as well as to long-term issues of overriding strategic importance.

Benchmarking never makes a principal issue of the "soft" factors of a company. Indeed, in our opinion these should never be a principal issue, but should be subordinate to the operational content of the business. Without successful business operations, there will be no workplace in which to exercise leadership or concern ourselves with management–employee relations. If we want to make an organization more business-oriented and make the people in it more aware of what is essential, benchmarking is an admirable instrument for the purpose. If we start from the customer's standpoint and impress that on the organization, it will focus its attention on satisfied and profitable customers. That *is* a principal issue.

Benchmarking strikes a balance between stability and renewal. It gives opportunities to study how other organizations have made their processes and functions successful. This supplies clues to what needs to be changed, but also to what should be kept intact. We must never forget that even successful business units have concealed inefficiencies within themselves. Conversely, even less successful organizations may harbour a large number of functions and processes that are performed with high efficiency.

One of the outstanding advantages of benchmarking is the learning process that it gives rise to, even in areas where no learning was thought needful. There is an old American adage which says, "Don't mend it if it ain't broken". The philosophy behind it is that one should not strive for pre-eminence or excellence, but be satisfied with products and processes that seem to work.

In many organizations, however, if you look for the places where resistance to change is greatest, you will generally find that those are the places where benchmarking can do the most good.

To sum up, then, the benchmarking method focusses the attention of management where it ought to be focussed, on the operational content of the business. At the same time it focusses the attention of the employees on what is important to the operative and strategic success of the business. This promotes a strong sense of businessmanship and result orientation, with the result that learning takes place in those areas which are essential to both the business and its employees.

BENCHMARKING AS AN INSTRUMENT FOR IMPROVEMENT

We can specify the effects of benchmarking thus:

> Benchmarking identifies the manufacturing and other operations in an organization that need to be improved. The next step is to look for other organizations that perform equivalent operations with outstandingly good results and to make detailed measurements of how they do it. A process of improvement can then be initiated which aims at shifting the focus of the organization and developing the skills of its leaders and members.

Benchmarking goes far beyond traditional competition analysis. The latter typically comprises three avenues of approach:

1 Analysis of products and services in terms of costs and quality.
2 Economic analysis with reference to the overall economics of the competing system.
3 Analysis of the attitudes of customers, suppliers, etc. with a view to acquiring background information.

Competition analysis is often applied to structural business transactions, i.e. acquisitions and divestments. However, it is extremely rare to find such analyses being used as the starting point for an in-depth programme of improvement. People in many industries are fully aware of the differences that exist in various respects, yet this awareness does not lead to action on the part of the companies that lag behind. One of our own clients was a large engineering company whose relative cost position was weak compared to that of its chief competitor. Despite the fact that the company knew this, and had access to an analysis with facts and figures to confirm it, nothing had been done for a long time to remedy the situation.

Our interpretation of this phenomenon is that a base of facts alone is not enough to initiate and sustain the process of change that is necessary to bring about improvement. In other words, there is a lack of correlation between analysis and action. Our experience, moreover, is that benchmarking is the method that can directly link a solid base of facts to learning and action. Why, we may then ask, is benchmarking not used more often, when the method has long been known and its results must be judged as excellent? Let us suggest some possible explanations.

Firstly, there is a general tendency to regard one's own achievements as superior to other people's. In addition, there is a feeling that it is shameful and unworthy to imitate what others have done instead of developing one's own solutions. The prime characteristic of a learning organization is that it notes, learns and adapts successful behaviour, thereby laying a foundation on which to build up its own knowledge and skills. Sometimes it seems to be part of the Western macho ideal to want to do it all and know it all without help. This is an obstacle to setting up a learning process based on openness to the best existing solutions.

Secondly, people often have the idea that their own business is so specially unique that meaningful comparisons cannot be made. The leader often takes a kind of perverse pride in the culture of the organization, its unique traits and its historical background—factors which defy comparison between his own field or his own organization and anything else. This attitude, we think, prevents people from seeking and acquiring knowledge that could improve their own operations. If such an attitude prevailed in knowhow-intensive fields like management consultancy, progress would grind to a halt. On the contrary, acquisition of knowledge developed by others is essential to success, because the knowledge is used as raw material for intellectual processing to add value.

Thirdly, we have come across many companies with in-house analysis departments which are unfortunately populated by people whose level of ambition is too low and who are not rewarded for making a hard and progressive effort to improve the organization. The analyses they make of competitors and their own situation are thus bland and worthless. Integration of analysis and action to push for improvements needs to be intensified in many companies that have staffs paid to analyze markets, customer-perceived quality and competitors.

Fourthly, we often find that organizations are the prisoners of their own industry's peculiar culture and thus incapable of assimilating information from outside it. Analyses of competitors' behaviour seek to show what the competition has already done rather than what could be done. This reduces the value of analysis in varying degrees depending on how much of a closed shop the industry is. There are industries like medical care and publishing which are extremely introverted and disinclined to accept impulses from the outside world, while there are others like the aviation and automotive industries which are wide open to ideas from any source. There is thus considerable variation in what an industry perceives as its own mystique.

The question, then, is why there are so few successful benchmarking programmes around. It is true that benchmarking as an instrument of change begins with an analysis of the competition, but it does not end there. Whereas the focus of interest in competition analysis is almost always on comparisons of products and financial strengths, benchmarking goes on to consider the underlying operative content and the leadership skills that lay the foundations for success.

And whereas competition analysis is essentially limited to companies that sell and manufacture directly competing products and services, the benchmarking method can be applied without limit. It can, so to speak, find excellence in a given area in any field of endeavour, and apply the findings to its own situation.

Benchmarking, moreover, is applied by the people responsible for regular line management. It requires the active participation of the managers involved, and thus helps to generate the commitment that boosts the method to its demonstrated high degree of effectiveness. Traditional competition analysis, by contrast, is handled mainly by staff departments—a recipe for lack of impact and feeble efficiency.

Benchmarking—The Learning Organization— Developing Skills—Improving Performance— Result Orientation

Benchmarking derives originally from the productivity axis of the efficiency graph. Its basic function was, and still is, to reduce and close gaps, or to create a gap in one's own favour and achieve excellence. As the reader will understand, this function deals with easily quantifiable factors such as productivity relations, e.g. output as a function of resources consumed. The term resources here covers costs of all kinds, including capital costs, just as output may refer to goods or services of any kind.

Someone has said that anything which can be measured can be benchmarked, and nowadays practically anything can be measured. It is the value axis of the efficiency graph that has long been the stumbling-block. Approaches like cost-benefit analysis and value analysis have been based on the right ideas, but have been hampered by lack of analytical instrumentation for weighing, say, a given utility function in a service product against customers' willingness to pay for it. Nowadays it is possible and entirely feasible to do this.

Value analysis was pre-empted by engineers, especially in manufacturing industry. Cost-benefit analysis was likewise pre-empted by sociologists, often with distinctly leftward political leanings. Modern market analysis techniques have yet to be adopted by corporate managements in their assessments of value creation, but we are convinced that they will be so adopted on a large scale during the nineties. Thus far, however, modern techniques are still largely confined to market analysis departments.

One of the things that has surprised us most in our work with benchmarking has been its effects on the organizations concerned. The characteristic of a *learning organization*, according to Peter Senge of MIT's Systems Thinking and Organizational Learning

Program, is that leaders and other employees of the organization learn new things all the time. They must be allowed to make mistakes while doing so, but mistakes would be expensive if they happened in business or organizational reality, so Mr Senge uses simulations of various kinds alongside normal working routines to impart the desired lessons.

Another angle on the term learning organization, and an excellent one in our opinion, is the codification of successful behaviour noted elsewhere in the same or other organizations. Codification of a successful way of doing things upgrades the competence of the whole organization, whereupon a new platform is created to press on and develop peak skills, which in turn are codified and passed on.

The benchmarking method has proved uniquely suited to increasing receptivity to lessons on successful behaviour. It effectively cures the "not invented here" syndrome, inducing people to open their minds and shelve their conceit. Performance orientation is a good thing on the whole, but it can have some serious drawbacks. Sometimes people are so keen to prove themselves superior in all respects that they close their minds to new knowledge. Conceit flourishes. People think that they know best and can do everything best without assistance. If benchmarking can be used to introduce learning as an important component of performance, half the battle is won. By persuading people that being best means being constantly willing to learn and change, we can easily bring about the change to a learning organization that so many companies and other organizations desire. Thus in addition to the operative consequences of closing and eliminating negative gaps or opening positive ones, benchmarking also has the consequences of a cultural revolution. This latter element is extremely important and comes, so to speak, as a bonus with a well-implemented benchmarking process.

Developing skills can be defined as a symbiosis of four factors:

1 Knowledge, i.e. awareness of various elements of knowledge.
2 Motivation, i.e. the various forms of rewards and encourage-ment that make people want to learn.
3 Situation, i.e. opportunities for applying knowledge in a way that contributes to efficiency and success.
4 The will of the individual to develop his or her own knowledge.

Benchmarking provides uniquely fertile soil for development of skills.

In the first place it furnishes elements of knowledge from different environments, gathered by collection and analysis of data.

In the second place benchmarking supplies the motivation for a constructive drive for improvement. This assumes, of course, that the process involved in the benchmarking programme is properly planned and has full management backing.

In the third place the benchmarking method sets up a situation in which knowledge can be applied.

In the fourth place, finally, values are quickly implanted which combine efficiency and performance in a such a way that individual wills are guided in a direction that benefits the business. The effect, in other words, is to make the individual, the group and the company pull in the same direction. And that, dear reader, is no easy thing to accomplish with a single method.

Performance orientation and a will to achieve ever-better results are effects that most organizations in the nineties earnestly desire. Benchmarking focusses on performance at the expense of power and relations, though naturally these three things all overlap. Semantics, or the meaning assigned to words, varies from one person to another. In our experience, some people's eyes light up on hearing the words "learning organization", whereas others do not react to those words but are turned on by mention of skill development. We have used several of these terms in the hope that the reader will feel at home with at least one of them; we are however aware of the overlaps and semantic imprecisions that exist in all management terminology.

Leadership, according to Harvey J. Brightman, is an art, not a science. In science, he points out, you can quantify variables, derive formulae for interrelationships and determine optimum solutions. In leadership the variables are obscure, their inter-relationships unknown or unknowable, and you look for satisfactory solutions. In short, leaders must often use judgment rather than analysis in making decisions. Good judgment, however, demands a measure of mental competence which often exceeds our intuitive ability.

Our definition of performance is action taken with a view to promoting the short-term and long-term efficiency of the business. This means that we are talking about both operative and strategic efficiency. As the world becomes increasingly performance-oriented, organizations of widely varying kinds will strive to enhance their performance and efficiency. Benchmarking is an excellent tool for the purpose, especially for organizational units which are not exposed to competition and whose performance is thus not measured by a profit-and-loss account. This naturally applies in large measure to the public sector, but the argument applies equally well to staff functions in companies and other organizations. The efficiency of staffs, i.e. the value they create in relation to their productivity, is often insufficiently known. Benchmarking of staff units is a way to overcome this problem.

We would also like to say a little about leadership development in relation to benchmarking. We have been involved in scores of leadership development programmes where we have lectured on strategic and operative skills. It gradually dawned on us that such lecturing is like teaching people to swim on dry land unless we have access to material from the participants' own working environment. In this context there is a way of using fact bases and benchmarking that we have found effective:

1 Start on an aggregate level by discussing the development of the industry concerned and the company's position within it.
2 Take case histories from the company itself. In a bank, for example, we can apply benchmarking to a number of branch offices.
3 Let the participants themselves, in the course of the programme, set up or actually operate a benchmarking project.

This achieves the two important objectives of a leadership development programme, viz. both entertainment value and substantial value. Otherwise there is a risk that the knowledge-intensive parts will be too dull, and the light relief parts will impart too little knowledge.

For these reasons we would like to recapitulate the sequence *strategy formulation—strategy implementation—leadership development—training*.

A constant struggle seems to prevail between the engineers and economists responsible for operations on the one hand, and

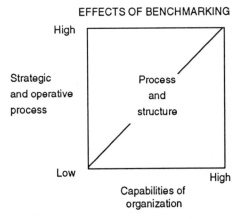

Figure 3 *Benchmarking contributes both to enhancement of skills and to improvement of the operative content of work*

behavioural scientists concerned with individuals and organizations on the other. This struggle is reminiscent of the dispute about the chicken and the egg.

Figure 3 illustrates the dilemma. Should one start by training the organization in group dynamics and individual psychology, or should one concentrate instead on the company's strategies and operative objectives?

As the reader will appreciate, neither of these alternatives is optimal by itself. The thing to do is to try and develop the quality of operations concurrently with the organization and the individuals in it. Many people have been saying this for decades, but few have succeeded in doing it.

Benchmarking is in fact an approach that works exceptionally well here. It links group dynamics and individual development directly to both the short-term operative content of the business and its long-term strategies.

Benchmarking in Practice

Before we embark on the actual description of the method, we would like to point out some of the success factors to be borne in mind, and pitfalls to be avoided, in benchmarking. Let us first list some of the errors and pitfalls that we have encountered in our own experience or learned from the experience of others.

To begin with, there is a danger that benchmarking may stop at a mere analysis of key indicators without leading on to the massive and penetrating attack of which the method is capable. The process of change and learning that it makes possible must not be squandered away because the approach to it is too narrow or too shallow.

Benchmarking projects are often launched in too much of a hurry with too little preparation. If somebody is told to set up a benchmarking exercise and have it finished by the end of next month, it is usually a waste of effort.

Most benchmarking groups realize at an early stage in the proceedings that accounting systems do not provide the information they need with the requisite precision. Here it is important to be able to apply ABC (Activity Based Costing) analysis or some other method of breaking down a cost mass or quality assessment into its component parts for purposes of analysis.

It is essential to proceed from customers' needs, and also to interpret customers' wishes correctly and then make any necessary corrections to enhance the impact of the benchmarking process.

A common mistake, however, is to make the approach too broad. If the need is not exploratory or diagnostic but action-oriented and therapeutic, it requires a high degree of goal orientation. Trying to encompass all functions at once is often an inefficient way of doing it.

As with any tool of management, there is a risk of the method being touted as a doctrine of salvation to the exclusion of all others. Although we have found that benchmarking possesses a great deal of substance and is highly effective, there are of course many situations where it is not at all the best approach.

Many people also fall into the trap of paralysis through analysis. The actual process of collecting and analyzing data fascinates them so much that they cannot leave it and go on to progressive implementation of change. The situation is the turning point here. In some situations the crucial thing is to recognize the facts, while in others it is the ability to move from insight to action that is critical.

Benchmarking can sometimes be crippled by pressure of acute day-to-day problems and intra-organization politics. If a progressive benchmarking exercise is in progress when something dynamic happens in the outside world, there is a risk that all hands will rush to man the pumps, postponing the project until later. Again, it may be a politically sensitive matter for power-oriented people in an organization to conduct an honest and possibly revealing benchmarking project. So it sometimes happens that a good start is derailed, usually to prevent truths being revealed that might be embarrassing to somebody.

A cascade approach to benchmarking is recommended. It is advisable to start fairly broadly, without going into too much depth, to explore and identify "suspects". Then you can proceed to more action-oriented benchmarking in depth to accomplish concrete improvements.

The measurements that result from a benchmarking process in terms of costs, time and quality are seldom very complex. A single measure of productivity is cost per unit produced. Let us not forget that lead times and many other parameters are derived from the main measurement of productivity, which may be expressed as number of units per pound of cost or cost in pounds per unit.

CUSTOMER-PERCEIVED QUALITY VERSUS NORM-RELATED QUALITY

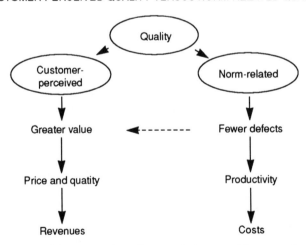

Figure 4 *Customer-perceived quality can help you either to sell more units at the same price or to charge a higher price for the same volume. This affects the revenue side of the profit-and-loss account. Norm-related quality, on the other hand, is connected with the zero-defect philosophy, quality costs and the productivity aspect. Minimizing defects naturally influences customer-perceived quality (dashed arrow pointing left). However, compliance with norms or standards primarily affects the cost side of the profit-and-loss account*

Similarly, in our opinion, measurement of quality should not refer solely to rejects, defects and wastage arising from the production process. Correct benchmarking of quality should moreover be based on customers' needs broken down into utility functions and the organization's ability to satisfy those needs in comparison to its competitors. This is a complicated and laborious process, but one which in our opinion reveals a true picture of the businessmanship we are striving for.

The term quality is complicated because it is interpreted differently by marketers and engineers. Figure 4 illustrates the difference between customer-perceived quality and norm-related quality. A well-run benchmarking exercise stimulates an organization to improve its ability to solve problems. By identifying the problems the organization is forced to think things all the way through, which stimulates creativity. Creativity is defined here as the ability to integrate known elements of knowledge in new and innovative ways. Benchmarking supplies the elements of knowledge that are needed to pursue a forward-looking, creative process of development.

One great mistake is to treat benchmarking as a one-off effort and neglect to follow through all the way into a steady state in order to achieve the desired effect, which is to create a learning organization that produces better results.

The more we work with benchmarking, the more clearly we see its advantages as an instrument for bringing about cultural changes in organizations. Persistence in using the method teaches lessons that will be beneficial for a long time to come.

We have yet to encounter a department which, after an initial review, claims that it has nothing to learn. Benchmarking thus prepares people mentally to make quite radical decisions such as a make-or-buy analysis, i.e. to determine whether they should really be producing and delivering a service themselves, or whether it has lost its meaning over the years. Does it actually have anything to offer customers? Has productivity deteriorated? The make-or-buy question is likely to be one of the most important issues to consider during the remainder of the nineties.

Now let us get to the method itself.

2
Aspects and Categories of Benchmarking

Before we move on to the actual mechanics of implementation, we need to discuss the various aspects and categories of benchmarking. Although benchmarking has been presented as a tool, the models and aspects that are a function of its application are of course strongly influenced by the individual situation.

Quality, Productivity and Time

Though we are aware that reality is both composite and complex, we have nevertheless opted to make an analytical distinction between benchmarking of quality, productivity and time. The *quality* aspect comprises the business of delivering value to customers, regardless of production cost. Quality is one component of customer-perceived value, but so is the price or sacrifice of resources that the customer has to pay to obtain the product or service. *Productivity*, on the other hand, is the business of producing a given volume with the minimum input of resources. The value the customer puts on what is produced is not the focal point in the latter case. The third parameter in the heading, *time*, is a very useful unit for expressing both productivity and quality. If we wanted to be absolutely stringent in our analysis, time would not have a heading of its own but would be included as a subcomponent of productivity and, to some extent, of quality. However, since the concept of time has acquired such weight as a measurement of performance, we have decided to treat it as a separate entity.

Categories of Benchmarking

Seeking excellence in the world around us is a highly relative business. The excellence we can find depends to a high degree on the horizon we can view. Analytically, we can distinguish between three categories of benchmarking.

- *Internal benchmarking* refers to comparisons made within the same organization, e.g. between subsidiaries, branches, sales groups, etc.
- *External benchmarking* makes comparisons with similar operations elsewhere, such as competitors and colleagues in other countries.
- *Functional benchmarking* is the third and perhaps the most exciting category. Here the comparison is made between functions or processes in different industries. The idea is to seek excellence wherever it may be found.

Which of the three categories you choose depends on the situation and on where the best benchmark is to be found.

QUALITY

In the first chapter of this book we discussed the meaning of value and quality and tried to explain the terms in their historic context. The concept of quality has assumed a very prominent place in present-day companies and organizations as a tool for improvement in their development programmes. The term quality can be defined from two standpoints. The first is that of the customer; here quality development is a tool for satisfying customers' needs and expectations. The second is that of internal production engineering, where the company sets itself quality standards so that it can keep up the standard of quality that customers expect.

The wave of quality development techniques now sweeping over the industrialized world has its origins in Japanese quality thinking. The concept of quality has been an important element in Japan's global industrial expansion. In recent years the industries of North America have sought to counter the "Yellow Peril" with a similar weapon. They have launched a systematic quality drive under the device of TQM, Total Quality Management. For the past decade, TQM has been one of the hottest issues in North American management circles, and now it is in process of gaining a firm foothold in Western Europe too.

TQM is a tool for focussing the energy of an organization on the quality content of its operations. A prize called the Malcolm Baldrige National Quality Award was instituted a few years ago; it is awarded to those companies which, according to its statutes, have been most successful in pursuing their quality programmes. This quality prize is connected with benchmarking in two interesting ways. Firstly, all prizewinners undertake to share their knowledge and experience with other American companies, and secondly, a full quality points score is conditional upon the use of benchmarking!

The TQM concept is now firmly entrenched in the American business world, and Donald Peterson, former Chairman of Ford Motors, speaks of TQM as "the method that has started America's recovery with national co-operation as one of its greatest strengths". In common with all doctrines that achieve some degree of success, the TQM philosophy of quality has not escaped criticism. The most cynical critics point to the fact that the winners of the award are by no means numbered among the most financially successful companies in the United States in the past few years. The list of recent winners includes General Motors, IBM and Westinghouse Electric, for example—none of which have lately been the darlings of Wall Street.

The Malcolm Baldrige National Quality Award is quite simply America's way of facing up to the industrial might of Japan.

The term quality is used rather loosely in a business context. To counteract this lack of semantic rigour, we reproduce below the description of quality published by the Swedish Institute for Quality Development. This institute, incidentally, offers its own annual National Quality Award to the Swedish company or administration which, according to its assessment procedure, is judged to have the most excellent quality. The SIQ has kindly given us permission to quote its basic criteria of quality.

Basic Criteria

A deliberate effort to develop quality results in higher productivity, more satisfied customers, better profitability and increased job satisfaction for all employees. Quality is achieved through systematic work to satisfy customers' explicit and implicit needs. The Swedish Quality Award is based on a model of evaluation that can be used by organizations of all kinds. The model is a powerful aid to the work of quality development. Its basic criteria are these:

Customer orientation

The goal of all organizations is to satisfy customers' explicit and implicit needs. All members of the organization must regard it as their duty to satisfy both external and internal customers.

Leadership

A personal, active and visible commitment on the part of every leader is essential to creating a culture that puts the customer first. The most important task of leadership is to set goals and create the right conditions for every subordinate.

United participation

Creation of a successful organization requires the participation and collaboration of every member. Everyone must therefore be aware of the goals, be furnished with the necessary means and be informed of the results achieved.

Skills

The competitiveness of an organization is founded on the skills of its members. To make progress, the skills of every member must be developed in a direction that strengthens both the individual and the organization.

Long view

The operations of the organization must be evaluated in relation to long-term goals, not to short-term advantage. Investment in quality development leads to higher productivity, higher market shares and higher profitability in the long view.

Social responsibility

As a part of society, every organization and its members bear a social responsibility. This means not just complying with current laws and regulations, but also making a constant effort to do better.

Process orientation

The operations of the organization are to be viewed as a process that can be divided into a number of subprocesses and support processes. These must be identified and form the basis of responsibility and authority.

Preventive measures

It pays to prevent faults in products and processes, and it is also essential to call upon outside expertise for this task.

Constant improvement

Constant improvement of goods, services and processes is needed to attain and maintain maximum profitability. This view must permeate all operations and all members of the organization.

Learn from others

The organization must constantly seek to learn from others in all areas so that it can further develop its operations. It is important to compare oneself with the organization that is best at a specific process, regardless of what industry that organization belongs to.

Faster reaction

Shorter response times, shorter lead times and faster reaction to changes are crucial to all operations. This applies to development, production and delivery of goods and services as well as to administrative processes.

Fact-based decisions

Decisions must be based on documented, dependable facts. Every member must be assured of the opportunity to measure and analyze facts that affect customer satisfaction and productivity.

Collaboration

Collaboration is a key issue in a successful organization. Collaboration must embrace customers, co-workers, suppliers, owners and society at large.

Thus under the heading "Learn from others", TQM (and, as we have seen, its Swedish counterpart SIQ) recognizes benchmarking as an important tool of quality development in organizations. This recognition is important in two ways. Firstly it helps to promote benchmarking as the powerful tool for result improvement which in fact it is, and secondly it identifies award winners as excellent benchmarking partners—especially since by entering the quality award competition they have undertaken to share their knowledge and experience.

It would go beyond the purview of this book to discuss whether the Malcolm Baldrige National Quality Award and its equivalents elsewhere are the best and only way to promote quality consciousness, but they do share with benchmarking the strength that they strongly focus attention on the operative content of business.

Quality and Benchmarking

In the introduction to this book we noted that the purpose of all organized activity is to create a value which is greater than the cost of producing it. This means that quality is not an end in itself, but simply a means of setting up a system which is optimally capable of delivering value. People, information and processes in an organization must be systematically united to create such a system. Benchmarking is an exceptionally powerful instrument for discovering and learning how other organizations have built their quality systems. From the quality standpoint, benchmarking can be used for several purposes:

- Customer-perceived quality.
- Norm-related quality.
- Organization development.

A customer is defined as a person who makes decisions about buying. Thus customers may be found both within an organization, placing orders with other departments, and outside it, as end users. The value that the customer feels he is getting from his supplier must be on a level that satisfies his needs. He must feel that the value he is getting is worth at least as much as the money he pays or any other sacrifice that he makes to get it. Where deliveries are made to an outside customer, the latter often has a number of alternative suppliers to choose from. This, however, is not the case with most internal supplier–customer relationships. Here the normal market mechanisms are totally absent, and it is here that benchmarking is most effective as a stimulant to market-type transactions.

The focus of a benchmarking exercise aimed at improving customer-perceived quality can be directed towards a number of areas; some examples are listed below.

Customer-Perceived Quality

Customer Relations

How do companies and organizations whose quality behaviour is excellent handle their customer relations? What steps do they take to satisfy their customers' needs and consolidate their relations? How do they measure customer relations? What yardsticks do they use to measure levels of service, and how do they use the measurements to constantly refine their operations and achieve ever better quality in their customer relations? What systems do they use to win and keep customers who ask for help or have complaints?

Customer Satisfaction

The idea of customer-perceived quality is of course to keep the customer satisfied in all respects. What do really successful companies do to stay constantly one step ahead of the customer and find out how satisfied their customers are? How do they segment their markets? What methods of measurement do they use, and how are the measurements translated into action?

Comparisons with Competitors

How does your benchmarking partner systematically cope with his relative competitive position in his own area of operations? What trends and levels of indicators are used to identify satisfied or dissatisfied customers with reference to competitors?

Norm-Related Quality

The term norm-related quality refers to systems designed to assure delivery of quality that matches predetermined specifications and standards. Norm-related quality thus describes the levels which the organization's principal and support activities must attain to minimize the risk that the customer or user will be unsatisfied or dissatisfied. Examples of areas to which internal or norm-related quality applies are as follows.

Development Processes

How are development and design processes organized to ensure that the goods and services being developed and improved will satisfy customers' quality requirements? How are customers' requirements translated into quality standards? What systems exist to shorten development lead times?

Production and Distribution Processes

What does the organization do to ensure that its production and distribution processes are designed to deliver value to customers while at the same time minimizing lead times, rejects, etc.? What methods and measurements are used, and what action is taken if any deviations from norm-related quality are detected?

Support Processes

Examples of support processes are finance, accounting, preventive maintenance, personnel administration, public relations and other administrative services. These are not part of the principal business of the organization as such; they exist solely to support the principal business. How do we identify what support processes are needed, and how do we measure and monitor their performance? How can support processes be developed and simplified, for example to shorten lead times?

Organization Development

The term organization development refers to activity aimed at creating an organization qualified to deliver high-class external and norm-related quality. Some examples of suitable areas for organization development benchmarking follow.

Operative Content

One of the many characteristics of successful companies is that their organization focusses strongly on performance and on the operative content of what they do. What kind of system and what control routines have they used to achieve this? What incentives are there to get away from power-oriented behaviour?

Human Resource Development

How is personnel planning linked to quality development? Personnel planning covers such items as areas of responsibility, development of skills, reward systems, co-operative goals, training and so on. What guidelines have been laid down, for example, for recruitment, introduction, continuation training, and is there a programme for human resource development aimed at quality enhancement? Human resource development also includes activities outside actual work assignments, such as preventive health care and social activities.

Involvement and Commitment

How does the successful company set up systems that encourage involvement and commitment on the part of employees to reaching the company's goals? Is there, for example, a system of development groups, suggestions, and so on? How is the involvement of the organization in quality and development measured?

Training

Companies that are successful in the area of organization development often have very well structured and smooth-running training packages. What do these look like, and what factors have they focussed on? How is training linked to the organization's overriding goals and strategies? What kind of measurements are used to evaluate training programmes? How do they verify that training results in better performance and motivation?

As we see, quality covers a large part of a company's or organization's activities. The whole system, or any part of it, can be benchmarked. You can make the selection according to what suits your own organization best or what is most conducive to satisfying customers' requirements.

PRODUCTIVITY

Benchmarking of productivity is a hunt for excellence in the areas that control input of resources. In this sense, input of resources has nothing to do with the value that the customer gets (cf. the example of the Trabant cited earlier). Productivity can be expressed as the quotient between volume of production and consumption of resources; the resources used may be costs or capital.

Figure 5 illustrates the relationship in the form of a productivity graph. If you are in the upper left quadrant, i.e. if you have a high volume of production and a low input of resources, your productivity is high. If on the other hand you are in the lower right quadrant, with a low output relative to input, the productivity of your operation is low.

The attentive reader will certainly have noted that the above section on quality had little to say about the ability of the operation to generate a surplus. High quality is to be regarded primarily as a means of delivering customer-perceived value, whereas productivity represents the steps taken to minimize the input of resources needed to produce the value.

Benchmarking is a very powerful aid to finding ideas and learning from companies and organizations in the world around

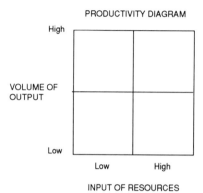

PRODUCTIVITY DIAGRAM

Figure 5   *Even if productivity is high, i.e. even if you are producing a large volume for a low input of resources, this does not necessarily mean that what you are producing is valuable to customers. Measurement of productivity by itself is therefore most relevant to products and services of a commodity nature*

you that exhibit exceptionally high productivity. The method is thus an excellent way to rationalize your cost mass, especially in times of recession. Figure 6 illustrates a productivity benchmarking study in a Central European office electronics company. The study comprises comparable products from three manufacturers, Alpha, Beta and Gamma. In this example we have divided the value chain into three main components: product, installation and service. The benchmarking study was initiated by the Alpha company, whose competitors Beta and Gamma served the same market.

The figure shows that Alpha's profitability is lower on the service side. The reason for this was that Alpha lacked an after-market culture in the modern sense; it regarded service as a necessary evil rather than as a business opportunity with the potential for selling extra equipment, spare parts and service billed by the hour. In addition, Alpha's product had been plagued by technical bugs which had adversely affected service profits although the fault lay in the product itself.

The study provided Alpha with a number of tools for upgrading its productivity with the help of its benchmarked competitors, Beta and Gamma. Both the latter were also very interested in learning how Alpha had managed to achieve such a low level of costs in its installation business.

Benchmarking is also an excellent aid to identifying opportunities for reducing capital commitment. Order processing,

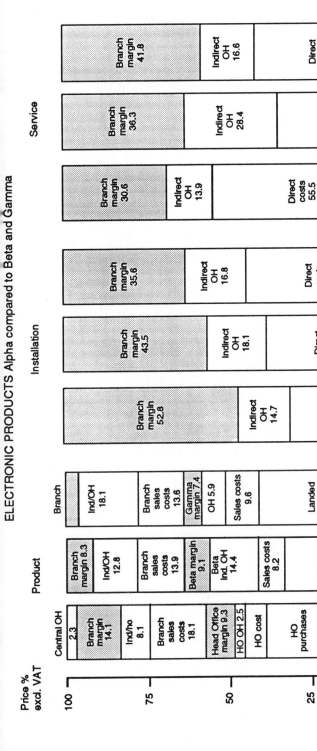

Figure 6 The bar charts describe the three main components of the business value chain: product, installation and service. Cost productivity per activity has been identified for each of these. The shaded area represents margin contribution

stock-keeping and invoicing routines, for example, are often generic in nature, not specific to a given type of industry. These areas thus make splendid candidates for benchmarking analyses because you can look far beyond the bounds of your own line of business. When the Rank Xerox Corporation in the United States decided to benchmark its stock-keeping function, it chose to study an American mail-order company, L. L. Beens. That company had an entirely different product mix and operated in a different industry, but the logic of the order processing, stock-keeping and invoicing routines was the same regardless of the products involved. L. L. Beens was a Best Demonstrated Practice company with regard to productivity, so this benchmarking exercise was of huge benefit to Rank Xerox.

There are naturally a number of different yardsticks that can be used to measure performance in benchmarking productivity. One very useful method of measuring productivity at the aggregate level is to look at value-added productivity per employee.

Value-Added Productivity per Employee

To arrive at a figure for value-added productivity per employee, you simply subtract all purchases including overheads and operating capital costs from the company's gross total revenue. Then you divide the result by the number of employees. This gives you an expression of the value added that each employee produces, given the value of what is sold.

Value-added productivity is defined by the formula:

$$\frac{\text{Revenues} - (\text{Purchases} + \text{Overheads} + \text{Depreciation} + \text{Interest})}{\text{Number of employees}}$$

The definition of value added per employee is derived from the following elements:

1 Revenues   Operating revenues
2 Purchases   Purchase costs of a direct nature
3 Personnel   All personnel costs including taxes, social
                security charges, personnel amenities, etc.

4 Overheads   Operating overheads
5 No. of employees   Average number during a year
6 Depreciation   Planned depreciation
7 Interest   Interest on operating capital

Examples of the Uses of Value-Added Productivity

Benchmarking

Analysis of value-added productivity is a very powerful and useful tool in benchmarking against other organizations because of the high explanatory value of this concept. In a comparative analysis it enables you to pinpoint "suspect" unproductive activities quickly and with high precision.

Replacing Labour with Bought-in Services

If the number of employees changes as a result of buying services, for example as the result of a make-or-buy analysis, this will reduce the denominator of the formula; there will also be a corresponding reduction in the numerator because the service will show up instead as a purchase or overhead cost. This is a central analysis in connection with the question of whether or not a given service should be bought from outside the company.

Replacement of Labour by Automation

If the number of employees is reduced because an operation has been automated, this will be reflected in the value-added formula, which also takes account of capital costs in the form of capital depreciation.

The Du Pont Formula

Another very useful way of measuring the productivity of an operation is to express it as return on total assets. The

THE DU PONT MODEL

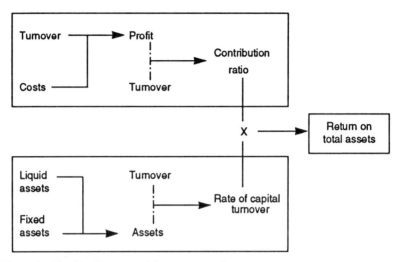

Figure 7   *The Du Pont model measures the return on the total assets of a business. It can usefully be applied to both whole businesses and parts thereof*

multinational chemical corporation Du Pont has given its name to a model which has proved highly serviceable. The Du Pont model starts with both revenues, costs and capital. Figure 7 shows how it is constructed.

The upper box in the model starts out with revenues and costs, where profit as a percentage of turnover represents the contribution ratio of the business. In the lower box the capital side of the business is set against turnover to give rate of capital turnover. By multiplying these quantities, you get the return on assets.

The Du Pont model lends itself admirably to studying both businesses as a whole and parts thereof. Using the model on a part of a business, however, requires that its capital side is identifiable. The risk inherent in using the Du Pont model is that the capital sides of different businesses may be valued according to different criteria. It is therefore necessary to know the method used for assessing capital values in order to be able to use return on assets and the Du Pont model to make comparative measurements.

The third method of benchmarking productivity, and perhaps the most useful of all, is to make an ABC (Activity Based Costing) analysis. This method has arisen out of recent developments in the field of product costing.

ABC Analysis

A new view of costing has emerged of late. The method is called Activity Based Cost Distribution, or ABC analysis. Certain circumstances have been highly significant to the emergence of this partly new approach to cost distribution. An important part of the background is that the growing complexity of industrial systems has gradually led to a proportionate reduction in direct material and labour costs, matched by an increase in the proportion of common costs. In earlier times, when direct material and labour costs made up the lion's share of total costs, it was quite feasible to distribute common costs automatically in proportion to the variable costs of individual items. Gradually, however, this principle of cost distribution has come to be seen as highly unreliable. Traditional principles of cost distribution have taken root and tended to go on being used as a matter of convenience. Changes in cost accounting involve

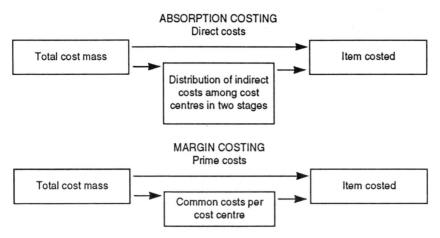

Figure 8   *In businesses with a substantial mass of overhead costs, neither absorption nor margin costing is an adequate instrument for precision measurement of results. Both models were devised at a time when overheads represented a much smaller proportion of the total cost mass than they normally do today*

questioning, reappraisal and all the other ingredients of a process of change.

To put it quite simply, the background was that indirect costs had come to account for a growing share of total costs. As a well-known accounting firm put it: "There used to be two bookkeepers to eight smiths. Now there are eight bookkeepers to two smiths". The result has been that standard products have tended to subsidize special products and services, and that high-volume products have subsidized items manufactured on a smaller scale. The traditional methods, absorption costing and margin costing, are illustrated in Figure 8.

The problem, as we see, is that reality is moving steadily farther away from the models as the complexity of business management grows greater. The corresponding diagram for ABC analysis is shown in Figure 9.

ABC analysis takes its starting point in the activities performed in a business and how these activities control the cost logic of the business. ABC analysis is a very powerful and useful calculation model to use as a base for benchmarking productivity. An ABC analysis is usually made with the focus either on products and groups of products, or on customers and groups of customers. Four elements must be defined within the framework of ABC cost analysis:

1 focus,
2 resources,
3 activities,
4 cost drivers.

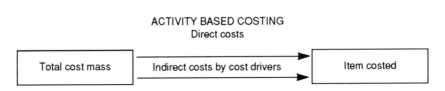

Figure 9   *With ABC, all costs are charged directly to the item costed. The idea of the model is that you identify and understand the activities that drive the costs of the business. This basic principle of ABC analysis is very useful for benchmarking productivity*

Focus

The focus of ABC analysis is the actual target of the cost calculation. In practice, as we said, it is often products/groups of products or customers/markets.

Resources

Resources are what do the work, generating costs in the process. Examples of resources are personnel, computer systems, production plant, and so on.

Activities

Activities are the work done by the resources, such as purchasing raw materials, writing invoices, drawing up budgets and making marketing plans. Activities can be defined in a large number of ways and may be more or less detailed. Although the resource element as defined above also includes hardware such as production plant, the term activity generally means human activity.

Cost Drivers

A cost driver is a quantity that links the activities to the focus which is the target of the ABC analysis. The number of manufacturing orders, for example, may be a cost driver. If a cost driver is to be usable in the analysis, it must be communicable, controllable, and accepted in the organization. The first step in an ABC analysis is to analyze cost drivers and their underlying activities. The facts can be elucidated concurrently, and the result depends to a high degree on how the ABC model is constructed with reference to aims and precision and, of course, on availability of relevant data.

The great value of ABC analysis is that it uses the underlying activities as a base to express the performance of the business.

It is thus the operative content of the business that determines where costs are booked. A classic example of erroneous costing is the case of high-volume and low-volume products. Say that a plant makes two products. One of them is made in large numbers, the other in small. The low-volume product requires more setting-up per unit and therefore consumes relatively more resources per unit produced. If the overheads are totted up and distributed according to a common volume-related index, the resulting product cost will be misleading. The high-volume product will be subsidizing the low-volume product because the booked share of overhead per unit is the same for both. ABC analysis corrects this by letting the underlying work content and the activities that control resources determine the cost distribution. This gives a truer distribution of overhead between high-volume and low-volume products.

Because ABC analysis, like benchmarking, uses operative processes and their underlying activities as a basis for analysis, it is an excellent and functional method to use for purposes of benchmarking too.

The ABC method can be used in the same way to analyze parts of a business—for example by expressing cost per invoice, cost per customer order, cost per customer account. The literature includes several books which describe the ABC analysis procedure in detail. As the reader will discover in the coming chapter on implementation of the benchmarking method, the views of business expressed in ABC analysis and benchmarking have many points in common, especially with regard to productivity, underlying operative content, and consideration of activities performed as the base. It is not however necessary to make an ABC analysis of the whole business to benchmark productivity; an ABC analysis is extensive and demanding. But if the business already is or has been the subject of an ABC analysis, then you get a large part of the internal analysis work of benchmarking into the bargain.

TIME

Time, like quality development, has come to symbolize the direction of industrial development in recent years. Fast flows in sales, administration, production, product development and distribution have received an increasing amount of attention as an important potential means of improving productivity and competitiveness. Time-focussed development programmes have demonstrated an almost spectacular ability to shorten lead times.

By studying the total time flow in a process you can get an overview of productive value-added time and unproductive non-value-added time. The latter often turns out to make up more than 90 per cent of total process time. In a complete delivery chain, say from sales negotiations to installation of a plant, value-added time often accounts for a very small percentage of total elapsed time. Figure 10 illustrates this graphically. The upper bar represents the calendar time occupied by a process; the dark areas are active time, and the white areas inactive time. In the lower bar we see that the number of active operations has been reduced and that the inactive intervals between them have also been shortened considerably. Making this kind of analysis of total process lead times forces us to adopt a holistic ear-of-corn-to-loaf-of-bread view.

The time aspect largely represents an expression of productivity and, to some extent, of quality. Throughput time should start when the customer places the order and run until the goods have been paid for. The same principle applies to internal processes within a company, such as product development or investment decisions.

From the decision point onwards, a lot of time is usually lost quite needlessly, costing visible amounts of money that contribute no value to the process. Setting value-added time in

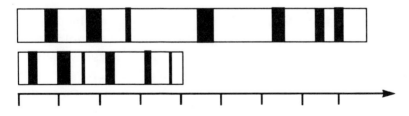

Calendar days

Figure 10 By shortening non-value-added time (white) and simultaneously shortening and reducing value-added operations (black) by rationalizing the work, you can substantially reduce the total throughput time

relation to available time is often a highly illustrative way of discovering how time is used in an organization.

Time compression efforts can be focussed on either external or internal customer relations. Faster throughput times are a parameter of customer-perceived quality because time is money to the customer too. Examples of time-related, customer-perceived values connected with ordering procedures include:

- quick response to requests for quotations,
- short delivery times,
- delivery free from hitches,
- quick installation and commissioning,
- short elapsed calendar time from enquiry to handover,
- speedy deliveries of spare parts,
- quick action to remedy faults.

In the large-scale perspective, too, there are striking examples of how time is used. One of them concerns the use of operating theatre equipment in Western European hospitals. The proportion of available time per employee varies widely from one country to another, but in countries like Sweden, Belgium and The Netherlands we can reckon about 1600 hours per person per annum after deducting vacations, sick leave and breaks. Hospital staff in Germany and the United States work many more hours in a year, not to mention those in Southeast Asian countries.

Benchmarking Time

Time, as we said, is an excellent unit for measuring the performance of an organization. Short throughput times contribute to customer-perceived quality, and most of all to productivity. Using time as a platform for benchmarking has proved highly successful. Everybody knows what time is, so there is seldom any difficulty in persuading people that shorter lead times are a worthwhile goal. Focussing on units of measurement related to throughput times gives great impact to flow-oriented thinking with reference to the often inter-departmental processes that take place in a business.

Many multinational corporations have successfully attacked the problem of lead times. Electrolux Cleaning Services, for example, has managed to cut delivery times for vacuum cleaner motors by over 90 per cent. In addition, they have improved quality and made savings on both guarantee and stock-keeping costs.

Another example is the ABB Group's global Customer Focus Programme. This aims at combining speed, flexibility and high precision in deliveries to customers, with the aim of halving all throughput times.

CATEGORIES OF BENCHMARKING

The focus of a benchmarking study, as we have said, may be either quality or productivity. The study may cover the whole of a business or parts of it; it may delve deep, or be confined to the aggregate level. We can use three categories of benchmarking to find excellence and meaningful points of comparison in the world around us.

Internal Benchmarking

Many businesses operate with some kind of branch structure. They may have a number of geographically scattered subsidiaries, divisions, service groups, and so forth. In such cases the business contains a number of similar operations that can easily be compared to each other. Benchmarking within one organization is called internal benchmarking. A sales company with offices in several European countries, for example, can compare them to find the Best Demonstrated Practice with regard to delivering customer-perceived quality. Another example is a large German food chain that uses internal benchmarking to identify potential cost savings in its business.

Running a benchmarking study is a splendid way to implement changes and teach your organization how benchmarking works. The organization can run benchmarking studies at its own pace and, as it learns how to use the method, sharpen its focus on the operative content of its work. With extremely few exceptions, it is always possible to identify opportunities for improvement by studying your own operations. Innovative processes may evolve and develop in a central system with a branch structure, and these processes can be adopted by other parts of the organization to the benefit of the whole. When the exercise takes place within your own organization you have automatic access to information and data; this means that the study can be completed sooner because you do not have to spend time and effort looking for and securing the co-operation of external benchmarking partners. Internal benchmarking, moreover, gives very high precision in the comparison when all the relevant data are collected from under the same roof. A weakness, of course, is that the chances of finding world-class performance in your own organization are less than if you look for outside alternatives. Nevertheless, internal benchmarking often leads to quick and substantial improvements in results.

Several companies and organizations that have used benchmarking over a period of time have made it standard practice always to start with an internal benchmarking project before going on to an external one—provided, of course, that the operation which is the subject of the exercise exists in more than one place within the organization. The knowledge derived from the internal project is then used as a base for continued benchmarking in an external perspective. This gives excellent opportunities for identifying and creating a model that can be tested and fine-tuned internally.

Internal benchmarking has the further effect of equalizing differences in performance between branches. Not only does the overall performance of the organization improve, but there is also less variation between parallel operations. Figure 11 illustrates schematically how precision in deliveries changed over a period of time in the four national subsidiaries of a European wholesale company in the textile business. Keen competition in the retail trade required the wholesaler to deliver to its customers eight times a year, and one of the retailers' most important requirements was that they could rely on the goods being delivered exactly when they wanted them, on a specified date.

The figure shows how the four subsidiaries, after applying benchmarking over a number of years, not only improved their individual performances but also converged towards a common,

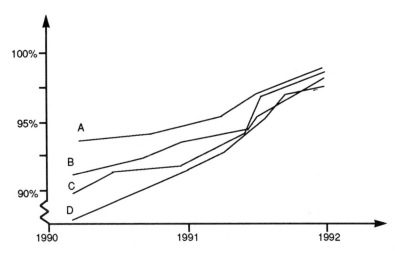

Figure 11   *Internal benchmarking helps not only to improve the results of the units involved, but also reduces the difference in levels of performance between them*

higher standard of precision. Over a period of time, then, internal benchmarking leads to better individual performance while at the same time the organization "closes ranks".

Finally, we should say a word of warning: do not underestimate the problems and difficulties of benchmarking just because it is an internal project. We have seen examples of how the difficulties can actually be exacerbated in internal projects by inertia and conflicts within the organization. Instead of concentrating on ways to make improvements, people have fallen to carping and defending their territory. Our advice in such situations is to press on methodically and patiently with the process of benchmarking, taking care to verify and check all data so that your detractors cannot quarrel with your findings.

Internal benchmarking is not intended as a substitute for external or functional benchmarking. It should be used as a first step towards attaining excellence in your business, and promoting learning and consensus with regard to the method.

External Benchmarking

External benchmarking means that you compare your organization with similar or identical organizations elsewhere.

Your benchmarking partners may be direct competitors, or equivalent organizations operating in other countries and serving other markets. The salient point about external benchmarking is the high degree of comparability between the organizations or functions involved.

The approach, however, will differ considerably according to whether you are benchmarking competitors in your own market or colleagues in other markets. Establishing a benchmarking partnership with competitors can be very fruitful, especially for the purpose of positioning your own company in the market. What are your strengths and weaknesses, both as you see them and as customers see them? Although external benchmarking cannot identify true world-class performance either, it can give clues about the internal working relations of the businesses you study. Benchmarking of direct competitors is naturally conditional upon your being able to establish a dialogue with them. However, the problems of access are seldom of the same magnitude when the focus is on an opposite number operating on a different market. National postal and telecom services, for example, routinely collaborate with each other on benchmarking.

The high degree of comparability that normally characterizes external benchmarking means that the degree of professionalism can be exceptionally high too. Operative content and processes can be benchmarked with precision and in-depth expertise.

In some respects, businesses in competition have a clear interest in being able to benchmark each other. This applies especially to operations which are peripheral to their core business, such as the function of purchasing commodity-type materials; here there is a common interest in improving productivity. In other cases, where the subject of benchmarking is of a more sensitive nature, the reverse applies. Do not be in too much of a hurry, but let the process take its time so that everybody involved in the benchmarking study feels comfortable with it.

The risk of external benchmarking between competitors is that it tends to focus on competition factors instead of seeking to identify excellent performance. It is an unaccustomed situation for many people to "dance with the enemy". The launch of an external benchmarking project may thus be preceded by heated internal discussions before the decision is made.

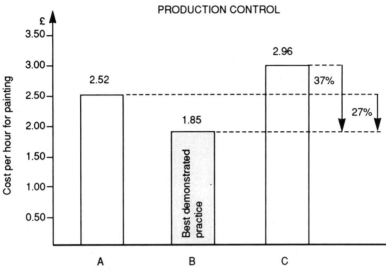

Figure 12 *The bar chart compares performance expressed as cost per hour for painting. To close the gap to the company with the Best Demonstrated Practice (B), it is necessary to identify and analyze the procedures and work processes that B uses*

Figure 12 shows a comparison of hourly production control costs between three large competing painting firms. Company B proved to have considerably lower costs than the other two.

Having noted that company B does the job at lower cost, the next step in the benchmarking study is to try to understand why and learn lessons from this.

Functional Benchmarking

Functional benchmarking is a comparison of products, services and work processes with those of top companies regardless of what business they are in. The object is to identify ideal behaviour wherever it may be found. When using other industries as references you cannot normally make comparisons on a fully aggregate level. The idea is rather to benchmark parts of businesses—work processes and suchlike—which display a logical similarity even in different industries. A European banking group, for example, might want to benchmark its standard of over-the-counter customer service against an organization of acknowledged excellence in this area, such as Singapore Airlines. Another example is a development engineering company in the telecommunications business that benchmarks Japanese automotive companies with reference to design and product development processes.

We use the word functional here because benchmarking on this level is often concerned with specific activities or functions in an organization. An alternative term that is sometimes used is generic benchmarking, where the word generic is used in the sense of "unbranded". This closely reflects the basic notion of functional benchmarking, which is to take excellence as a standard of comparison wherever it may be found.

If you have set up a benchmarking team and imbued your organization with a receptive, performance-oriented spirit, you will find great potential for breakthrough-class success in functional benchmarking, for it can give you new insights and new knowledge that can lead to radical changes in your operations. In short, it is functional benchmarking that offers opportunities for moving up into the world class. Companies and organizations which have worked extensively with benchmarking regard the functional variety as the "very essence" of benchmarking. Though both the internal and external categories hold potential for substantial and powerful improvements, it is in functional benchmarking that the full power of the method can be utilized.

Figure 13 is a schematic illustration of lead times from sale to delivery in two companies in different industries. The height of the columns represents the total time in calendar days occupied by the process. The Sauger company manufactures and delivers turnkey sound systems to the entertainment industry, and has concentrated hard for many years on achieving short lead times. Wallin Industries manufactures and delivers prefabricated dwelling houses with the same turnkey concept as Sauger. Wallin Industries identified Sauger as the company with the Best Demonstrated Practice with reference to short lead times in the manufacture and delivery of system products. Although these two companies differ almost diametrically in what they produce, benchmarking makes it possible to transfer Sauger's excellence in the matter of short lead times to Wallin Industries.

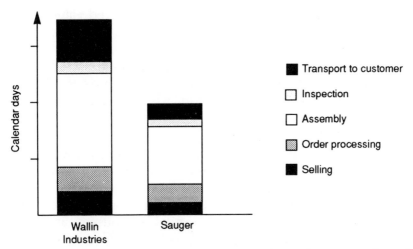

Figure 13 *Functional benchmarking lets you seek excellence regardless of where and in what industry it is exhibited. This bar chart compares the throughput times of an electronics company (Sauger) and a builder of prefab houses (Wallin Industries)*

WHAT MAKES A COMPANY OUTSTANDING?

When one has spent a long time working with benchmarking in a wide variety of companies and industries, as we have, one cannot help making a number of general observations. Trade logic and knowledge of conditions in one's own industry are admittedly of great importance, but nevertheless we can discern some universal success factors that characterize excellent companies regardless of which industry they belong to.

1 *Focus on performance*
   The organization exhibits strongly performance-oriented behaviour on all levels and in all areas. All development is focussed on operative content, not on shifts in balance of power. The organization is flat, with a low degree of integration.
2 *Cost consciousness*
   The business has good control of its costs, including its capital costs. It has often used ABC (Activity Based Costing) analysis to control its cost mass with precision. It is also keenly aware

of which costs contribute to customer-perceived value (good costs) and which do not (bad costs).

3 *Close contact with customers*
   The organization measures and keeps constant track of what its customers think. It also uses ABC analysis to identify profitable and unprofitable customers so that it can "educate" the latter.

4 *Close contact with suppliers*
   Suppliers are allowed to participate in development projects and are chosen for their product development ability.

5 *Concurrent focus on improvement of quality and productivity*
   These two theoretically conflicting factors are made to work together in practice. Reducing capital commitment in stocks often results both in better precision of delivery and in fewer mistakes in filling orders.

6 *Utilization of state-of-the-art technology*
   Application of data processing technology, in particular, offers great opportunities for improvement. Successful companies are especially good at taking advantage of these opportunities through internal training and education programmes.

7 *Focus on core business*
   Successful companies concentrate on the areas which customers regard as important and which give them a competitive edge.

The above list of characteristics of successful companies makes no claim to being exhaustive. Each of the headings in the list could perhaps even be made the title of a whole book on the subject.

3
Implementation of Benchmarking

Benchmarking, as we have said, is a systematic process which aims at seeking excellence in the world around us in order to learn and adopt its operative content and processes so that we can raise our own organizations to championship class. From an intellectual standpoint the theory of the method is almost ridiculously simple, but we must not underestimate the energy, hard work and creative thinking that a benchmarking project demands. Knowing that we need to look around us to find areas of improvement wherewith to initiate, pursue and complete a structured benchmarking process, we have arrived by experience at a five-stage sequence that has proved successful in a large number of cases (Figure 14). In this part of the book we shall review, systematically and thoroughly, the steps and operations that lead to success according to our experience from a large number of benchmarking projects.

THE FIVE STAGES OF THE BENCHMARKING PROCESS

Decide what to benchmark · Identify benchmarking partners · Gather information · Analyze · Implement for effect

Figure 14

However, the substance and implementation of one benchmarking project are seldom exactly like those of any other, so at this point we wish to make the following comment: Use this description of the benchmarking model as a guide. Do not use all its component parts slavishly, but let the specific situation rule even if it may conflict with something in this book. Our purpose is to describe a practical way of doing things that can be a powerful tool for running benchmarking studies.

Benchmarking in Project Form

The daily work of companies and organizations usually takes place in a functional structure according to the type of organization adopted—the object, naturally, being to handle routine work in the most rational manner. Processes of change and development, however, frequently make it necessary to look for solutions that go outside the regular pattern of organization. The need for change often runs through the entire company and all its processes, involving several parts of its operations. We

PROJECT ORGANIZATION INCLUDING STEERING COMMITTEE

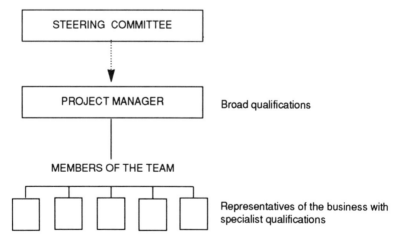

Figure 15 *A project group consists of a project manager and a number of members representing a specially chosen mixture of qualifications. The project manager reports to a client or a group of clients, who in the latter case may constitute a steering committee*

have therefore found by experience that a special project setup is a structure admirably adapted to benchmarking (Figure 15). When a task calls for a broad combination of qualifications, the project structure makes it possible to assemble a team of people with the right skills and the best chance of successfully completing the task. Setting up a project also gives the team a "licence" to operate outside regular channels without being hampered by organizational formalities. A further advantage is that you can co-opt specialists from outside your own organization.

The project form is thus admirably suited to the purpose because it creates a flexible and optimally composed *ad hoc* team. A further advantage is that being part of a specially chosen group often gives team members an extra energy boost and encourages them to think new thoughts. The variegated composition of the group also gives specialists and representatives of all parts of the organization an insight into each other's fields, resulting in cross-fertilization of ideas and the creation of synergies.

Make Demands on the Client

If you have commissioned a benchmarking project, you cannot just sit back and wait for the end result. If the project is to be successful, the person or persons who commissioned it must also take an active part in it. The client, or customer if you like, must be clear and specific in defining the terms of reference, aims and goals of the project. While the benchmarking project is going on, the client must be available for a number of working and review meetings, preferably in the form of a steering committee. The opportunity should be taken at such meetings to make any necessary corrections to the project. They can also be used to receive progress reports on how the work is proceeding.

Requirements for Project Work

The requirements cover, broadly speaking, understanding of the benchmarking project in terms of the results, goals, time schedule and resources that form the framework around which the benchmarking study is to be built. What problem areas or perceived needs for change in your own organization prompted the decision to seek comparison with the Best Demonstrated Practice elsewhere?

All our experience shows that it is always wise to spend plenty of time on planning the implementation of the project. Test, reject and revise different approaches to arrive at a project plan that offers a high likelihood of success.

This book presents a number of systematically ordered stages for launching and implementing a successful benchmarking project. But before you embark on these more concrete stages it is advisable to think through the scope and content of what you plan to do. What are the aims of the project, and what results do you hope to achieve? Is it your intention to deal swiftly with a problem of profitability by finding examples of effective and feasible ways to make substantial cuts in your organization's costs? Or is the benchmarking project part of a long-term strategy for an organization development process aimed at enhancing skills and creating a learning organization with the focus on performance-oriented behaviour? Are you scanning the world for excellence with a view to boosting customer-perceived value, or is it optimum resource management and higher productivity you are looking for?

What does your timetable look like? Is the end result more important than speed, or are you bound by time constraints such as scheduled budget discussions or the like? Whether or not you have a fixed deadline to meet, you should always draw up a timetable for your project.

What resources are available in the way of personnel and project budget? Determining what resources you need represents a large share of the work of getting the project off the ground. Estimates of requirements are always subject to some degree of uncertainty, and this makes demands on the planner. Nor can it be taken for granted that the best qualified people are currently available to work on the project. If experience of benchmarking already exists in your organization, it is invaluable and should if possible be incorporated into the project.

Members of the Project Group

The question of who should be involved in a benchmarking project is largely a function of what needs and aims have been determined (Figure 16). Sometimes a good case can be made for retaining

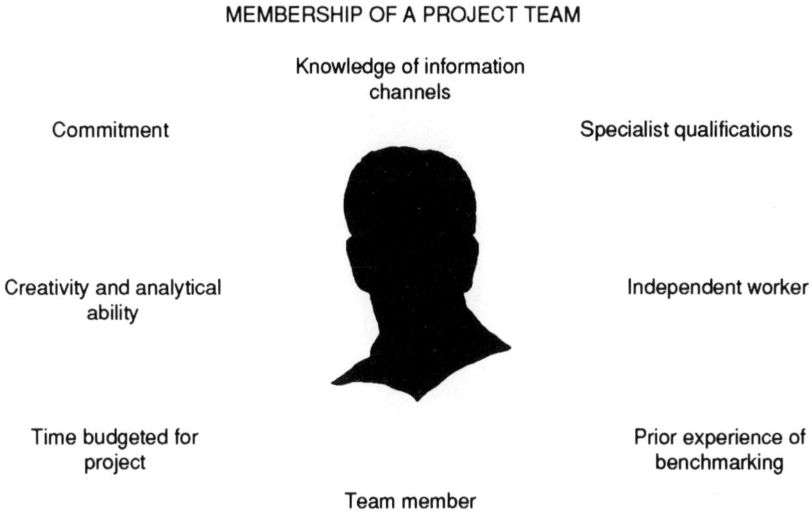

MEMBERSHIP OF A PROJECT TEAM

Knowledge of information
channels

Commitment

Specialist qualifications

Creativity and analytical
ability

Independent worker

Time budgeted for
project

Prior experience of
benchmarking

Team member

Figure 16   *The membership of a benchmarking project team should reflect a broad spectrum of qualifications and should include representatives of the organization under study*

outside consultants to do some of the work. They can contribute experience of benchmarking as a method, and have the further advantage that they are not involved in the internal politics of the organization. Otherwise the task will call for a major and committed effort on the part of people from inside the organization. An important requirement, regardless of the composition of the group, is for in-depth awareness of the trade logic of the industry you are operating in.

You should construct your group in such a way as to achieve an optimum mixture of people and a combination of roles adapted to the needs of the situation. The best solution in our experience, especially for an organization mounting its first benchmarking project, is to get the best of both worlds by setting up a mixed project group of in-house representatives supported by an outside consultant. This can generate a fruitful synergy between people who know the business thoroughly from the inside and "apolitical" outsiders with a detached view. Any outside consultant you retain must of course have solid experience and knowledge of benchmarking as a method. Later, when the organization has acquired hands-on experience of benchmarking, the need for outside representation will of course progressively diminish.

Here follows a list of considerations and criteria which you may find useful in selecting people for your project.

People Directly Involved

People employed in the areas to be benchmarked should always be well represented in a benchmarking project group. This is because it gives them an immediate opportunity to start learning lessons that can be applied in the subsequent process of change, and also because they can contribute their own specialized knowledge to the project. We have occasionally seen benchmarking projects run by a staff function or a consultant firm over the heads of the people concerned. This usually results in a report of dubious quality which is very hard to get accepted and acted on by the line organization. It is best if you can get the person in actual charge of the area concerned on the team. This will give the study great impact because the contents of the benchmarking analysis will be directly relevant to that person. A frequent problem here is the input of man-hours that benchmarking demands; the manager concerned may find it difficult to spare the time needed.

Mixture of Qualifications

Having a project manager with specialist qualifications for the job is one of the great strengths of an *ad hoc* project organization. As we said earlier, a project group can embody the resources and expertise with the best chances of guaranteeing success: people who know the business together with technical specialists, experienced benchmarking consultants, industry specialists, and so on.

Prior Experience of Benchmarking

If your organization has run benchmarking exercises before, you should try to get hold of somebody who has taken part, even if that person does not belong to the part of the organization which is the subject of the current exercise. The experience that the organization already possesses ought to be utilized. If none of your own people have any prior experience, you should consider co-opting an outsider who is an expert on benchmarking.

Commitment

It virtually goes without saying that the people you select should have a personal interest in and commitment to the project. Benchmarking requires both empathy and a lot of hard work if it is to succeed. If any of your candidates is reluctant to join the team, it is better to pick somebody else; ordering an unwilling individual to take part in a benchmarking project can be directly counterproductive.

Knowledge of the Company's own Information Channels

A large part of benchmarking consists in gathering facts about your own operations. A member of the project team who is familiar with the organization's information channels can therefore be a great asset. Here we put the broadest possible interpretation on the term information channels, i.e. we include support systems for sales, resource planning, order/stock/invoice processing, quality control, service, and so on. You can save much time and effort on a benchmarking project if you know where to seek and find in-house information. This knowledge can be of great value when it comes to analyzing external data together with your benchmarking partner.

Ability to Work Independently

Although a project-group organization implies teamwork, the members of the group must also be able to "run with the ball" on their own. Work on the project will not be very productive unless specific jobs can be delegated and responsibilities assigned to individuals.

Time to Work on the Project

It is important for members of the project group employed inside the organization to have the support of their own line managers so that time spent on the project does not conflict with their regular duties. It is the responsibility of line management to arrange matters so that the person concerned will not be torn between conflicting demands and loyalties.

Creative and Analytical Ability

A member of a benchmarking project team must have creative and analytical talents. Creativity is generally defined as the ability to combine existing elements of knowledge in new and innovative solutions, while analytical ability can be defined as the ability to interpret facts and draw conclusions from large volumes of information. As with much else, these talents represent a combination of innate aptitude and acquired experience. You do not need "supermen" to succeed in benchmarking, but a desire to understand relationships and find solutions is a great help.

The Project Manager

Project management is very much a situation-specific business; there are seldom any patent solutions to tell you exactly what the task involves. The project manager is responsible, within the agreed-on terms of reference, for supervising and leading the project and bringing it to a successful conclusion. He is not, however, responsible for securing the improvement in results that the benchmarking project is designed to accomplish; that responsibility must always rest upon the line organization represented by the client, or internal customer, whose needs the project has been set up to satisfy.

The role of project manager involves dealing with a series of situations that make widely varying demands.

Leadership

The project manager's main task is of course to lead the project team as a body along the road that leads to its set goal. Leadership of a project is a closer and more intimate kind of leadership than that normally required of a line manager. The role of project manager is a detailed, day-to-day business that calls for both precision and thoroughness.

Decision Making

A project manager has no command authority in the regular line organization. He should however be fully empowered to lead and make decisions about the project within given budget limits and directives. A project, and especially a benchmarking project, is often subject to heavy time pressure, which makes the ability to make quick and important decisions a key success factor.

Administration

Alas, even a benchmarking project requires a certain amount of administration to ensure its success: planning, setting up meetings, budgeting, scheduling and so on. There are a good many balls to be kept in the air. If the scope of the benchmarking project is extensive, it may be advisable to appoint a project secretary to relieve the project manager of routine chores.

Information

A project manager's responsibilities include the traditional information element, chiefly that of making regular progress reports to whoever commissioned the project. A further important duty is that of continually disseminating collected benchmarking data and checking their accuracy and relevance with parties outside the project team; this is an important part of facilitating and securing acceptance of the results of the study when the time comes for implementation.

Specialist Qualifications

Last but not least, it is obviously essential for the project manager to be fully familiar with both the benchmarking method and the area of operations which is the subject of the study. If you appoint a consultant or somebody else from outside to manage the project, it is very important to make sure that he or she is thoroughly versed in the trade logic of your business.

Problem Solving

When you run a benchmarking project you will be faced with a constant succession of problems that need to be solved. The nature and scope of the problems will vary widely, and you may sometimes have the feeling that no one problem is like another. But the great common denominator is that they can and must be solved. Finding your way through complex sets of problems nearly always demands a systematic approach to avoid getting bogged down in details and thus failing to find acceptable solutions.

Only rarely does the solution of a problem call for entirely new knowledge that must be obtained by basic research; the art of problem solving lies rather in systematic identification and compilation of a number of known facts which can then be put together in new, innovative combinations which lead to solutions. We generally use two basic models for problem solving, which we shall now briefly describe; each has its own advantages and drawbacks:

1 *Divergence–convergence*, in which you first diverge by sorting and breaking down all the elements of knowledge, and then converge by assembling the elements to reach new conclusions.
2 *The hypothesis approach*, which involves identifying the key issues of the problem and setting up hypothetical solutions which are then checked by research and analysis.

Divergence–Convergence

The "classic" approach of first breaking down a problem into all its component facts and studying them separately, and then reassembling them into conclusions and solutions, is the one which, experience suggests, is best suited to the purposes of a benchmarking project. The main steps in the method are:

1 *Thorough survey of the business*
Analysis of the present situation to identify and understand the business and its trade logic.
2 *Identification of problems*
Establishing consensus so that all are agreed on the nature of the problem. What is the problem, and what are the obstacles to solving it?
3 *Divergence (identification of elements of knowledge)*
What facts must be established to give us enough information to solve the problem effectively? We break down the business into its component activities and processes to acquire thorough, in-depth understanding of its operative content, trying as far as possible to separate discrete elements of knowledge. What factors are causing the problem, and how can they be described?
4 *Convergence (solving the problem)*
The critical step in the divergence–convergence method is the "turnaround" to reassemble all the elements of knowledge into a solution to the problem. The object is not just to solve the problem, but to find the *optimum* solution.

The divergence–convergence method has both advantages and drawbacks.

Advantages:
- The focus is on fact-based analysis.
- All aspects of the problem are taken into account.
- It gives opportunities for identifying optimum solutions.
- Thorough analysis helps the organization to accept the result.

Drawbacks:
- Can be time-consuming and expensive.
- There is a risk of getting bogged down in divergence at the expense of problem solving.

The Hypothesis Approach

The hypothesis approach to problem solving is based on the fact that in many problem situations there is a fairly firm notion of what the end result will be, in the light of acquired knowledge and experience. The task in such cases is to thoroughly analyze and confirm existing views rather than to come up with entirely new and innovative answers. The hypothesis approach is very widely used, especially by USA-based management consultancy firms. Its main steps are:

1 *Surveying the structure of the business*
   What are the factors that influence the business and the people in it? We try to understand the context and the culture in which the project is to operate. Typical elements of knowledge on the macro scale include market growth and dynamics, financial strength, competition, organizational structure and the efficiency (quality and productivity) of the business.

2 *Identifying difficulties and constraints*
   What factors narrow the options and constitute obstacles to problem solving and project work? It is important to identify and understand these factors at an early stage.

3 *Identifying critical questions*
   What issues are critical to the problem? What questions is the project intended to answer? Here we need a consensus of all interested parties on the nature and definition of the problem.

4 *Setting up hypothetical solutions*
   Hypothetical answers are proposed to the critical questions raised. Each hypothesis must (a) provide a comprehensive answer to a critical question, and (b) deal with the difficulties and constraints (see 2 above).

5 *Testing the truth of the hypothesis*
   Here we identify and list the arguments in support of the hypothesis. What underlying factors and arguments exist to prove the truth of the hypotheses we have proposed? First we construct a "logic tree" of postulates which we then examine and confirm by research and fact-finding. If a hypothesis proves fallacious, we backtrack and try to find alternative paths.

The hypothesis approach likewise has its advantages and drawbacks:

Advantages:
- It provides quick solutions to problems.
- It eliminates needless research and digging for information.
- There is often already an existing theory about the result.
- Construction of hypotheses puts a premium on knowledge and experience.

Drawbacks:
- The method is inadequate for solving complicated problems.
- There is a risk of "following the beaten track" and thereby missing new, ingenious solutions.
- Superficial analysis may make it harder to get the solution accepted by the organization.

Criteria for Success in a Benchmarking Project

Success in a benchmarking project depends upon a number of criteria which we have found by experience to be both relevant and essential. These criteria can be divided into "hard" and "soft" factors.

"Hard" Factors

1 *Frame of reference*
   Respect the frame of reference within which the benchmarking project is supposed to operate. In external benchmarking, especially, there is a temptation to wander away from the subject when talking to benchmarking partners in a new and fascinating environment.
2 *Schedules*
   Time schedules are made to be kept!
3 *Quality standards*
   It is important that the project should satisfy the client's needs and expectations.
4 *Budgets*
   However good the substantial result of a project may be, it is not justified if it costs more than was budgeted.

"Soft" Factors

1 *Spirit of co-operation*
Try to create a climate in which everybody is pulling in the same direction. The project should be characterized by "positive stress".
2 *Positive attitude*
Aim for change and be result-oriented. It is all too easy to get obsessed with nitpicking and prestige.
3 *Quality consciousness*
The commissioner of the project (client) should get something other than what he expected. "Excite and delight the customer."
4 *Commitment*
Commitment and entrepreneurship on the part of members of the project team are an extremely powerful driving force.
5 *Creativity*
Creativity, as we have said, is the ability to combine existing elements of knowledge into innovative solutions. This is of great value, especially for identifying and understanding potential in the operative content of excellent companies.
6 *Business ethics*
Benchmarking is *not* industrial espionage! Do not try to be "cunning". Confine yourself to asking questions that you would be willing to answer if they concerned your own organization. All participants must be agreed on the appropriate level of ethics.

Follow-up

Apart from the need to run a benchmarking project as a systematic, step-by-step process, there are a number of matters which come up over and over again at the follow-up and project evaluation stage, and which cannot be sufficiently emphasized:

1 *Win managers over to the idea of benchmarking*
Time after time we have seen vast resources expended on brilliant, fact-based analyses that have not led to any tangible results. In cultures which are not performance-oriented and where a spirit of prestige and territorial defence prevails, we

sometimes find a tendency to nitpicking instead of an open, eager willingness to absorb new knowledge. As an organization grows progressively more performance-oriented, these tendencies gradually fade away. Nevertheless, it is time well spent to organize a seminar or other form of briefing before the project starts in order to inform and persuade line managers about the benefits of benchmarking.

A question that is often asked at initial benchmarking presentations is: "How can we compare ourselves with somebody else? Our work is of a very special kind, and there is nothing like it anywhere else". This is seldom true in actual fact. When you set out to benchmark operations which are superficially very different, analysis of their component parts very often reveals the existence of more and more points of comparison and opportunities for improvement. If the managers and others involved (trade unions, for example) already possess the knowledge and insight that benchmarking is a powerful tool for identifying and understanding ways to improve operations and for creating a base of facts based on observed excellent performance elsewhere, then half the battle is already won. Benchmarking not only identifies excellent behaviour, but also proves by example that it is possible.

2 *Keep people informed of what is going on*

Thanks to the power and instructiveness of benchmarking, a study often results in remarkable, sometimes dramatic changes and developments in the organization concerned. Even where changes are beneficial, there is always a certain amount of anxiety and curiosity about what is happening. Outside consultants are particularly prone to neglect the need to keep top management and the organization as a whole constantly informed about the progress of their work. So in a benchmarking project, make it a habit to take time to issue regular news bulletins to all managers who are directly or indirectly affected by it. Regular news also has the knock-on effect of maintaining and increasing interest in and enthusiasm for benchmarking. Do not however be *too* ambitious about spreading information; encourage the recipients to *seek* knowledge of their own accord.

3 *Follow a simple, logical plan of action*

Work from a plan that sticks to a simple, step-by-step model which can be understood by all concerned. We have seen all kinds of benchmarking projects in the business world, comprising anything from three up to twelve stages. The important thing is not how many stages there are, but that the plan should follow a logical sequence without going roundabout ways to reach its objective. The five-stage model we recommend in this book is a general approach that has proved to work well in a large number of projects of varying scope and complexity.

4 *Document as you go*

Few projects are distinguished by being documented in too much detail or at too great length. The reverse is much more often the case. Running a benchmarking study involves collecting a great deal of information in the form of documents and data as well as transcripts of interviews and minutes of meetings. Give somebody the overall responsibility for co-ordinating and sorting documentation and keeping everything on file in one place. The same person can also double as project secretary and take notes at project group meetings, and so on. A little bureaucracy on this point can pay dividends in the long run.

The Five Stages of the Benchmarking Process

STAGE 1

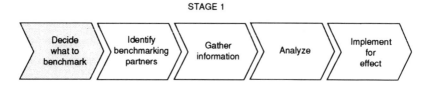

Figure 17

1 *Decide what to benchmark*

The first step in the benchmarking process is to proceed from the organization's (client's) need for benchmarking information. Will the exercise focus on customer-perceived quality or on productivity, and what are the critical factors for successful performance of the operation you want to compare? Any aspect of an organization's behaviour and performance can be benchmarked: goods, services, operative processes, support systems, staffs, costs, capital, customer-perceived value, etc. The ultimate objectives, too, vary widely: new strategies, planned cost reductions, focus on performance, new ideas, quality enhancement and so on.

STAGE 2

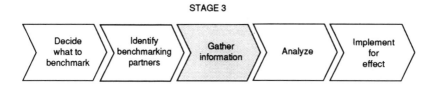

| Decide what to benchmark | Identify benchmarking partners | Gather information | Analyze | Implement for effect |

Figure 18

2 *Identify benchmarking partners*

Given the needs of your organization, where do you find the world champions? How can you identify those who represent the Best Demonstrated Practice and persuade them to collaborate on a benchmarking study? Good benchmarking partners, moreover, are not only excellent in their own fields but should also be comparable with your own organization to the highest degree possible.

STAGE 3

| Decide what to benchmark | Identify benchmarking partners | Gather information | Analyze | Implement for effect |

Figure 19

3 *Gather information*

This involves not only collecting hard quantitative and financial data, but also identifying and documenting the operative content, processes, etc. which explain and help you to understand the performance of the organization. The information-gathering phase calls for a painstaking, systematic effort to establish credible and useful benchmarks.

STAGE 4

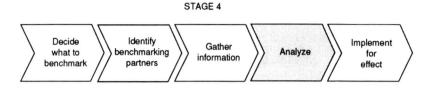

Figure 20

4 *Analyze*

The fourth stage is perhaps the one that makes the heaviest demands on creativity and analytical ability in the whole benchmarking process. Analysis means not only identifying similarities and differences, but also understanding the connections with the underlying operative content. It is further necessary to recognize factors which are not comparable and which cannot be influenced, for these too will affect the results of the analysis.

STAGE 5

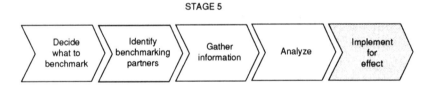

Figure 21

5 *Implement for effect*

The fifth stage involves not only putting improvements into practice, but also developing the organization and shifting its focus towards performance-oriented behaviour. The organization must set itself realistic goals based on the potential for improvement revealed by the benchmarking gap. These goals must be broken down, adapted to fit the regular structure of the organization and communicated to the people involved. How much time will this take, and how will the newly set goals affect the organization? A benchmarking project cannot claim total success until action has been taken to realize the potential for improvement and the desired results have been achieved.

Having assembled your project team, it is time to embark on the exciting venture of putting the benchmarking process into practice in your own organization. There will be periods of triumph and adversity. Project work is somewhat manic-depressive by its very nature, and you will veer between black despair and a euphoric feeling of success.

The chapters on implementation are written in such a way as to serve as both a practical guide and a work of reference which you can consult as needed. But before you actually start the project, read the chapters on the five stages of the benchmarking process and discuss them with your colleagues.

4
Stage 1: Decide What to Benchmark

STAGE 1

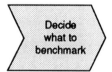

Figure 22

The object of the first stage is to identify what needs to be benchmarked in your organization by analyzing and understanding your customers' needs as well as the processes of your business and its operative content.

The whole organization can be benchmarked, as can its component parts, either from the internal standpoint of productivity or from the external standpoint of customer perceptions. You can run benchmarking exercises on products, sales, production lines, customer service, quality systems, work routines and so on. There are in fact no limits except those set by customers' preferences and the needs of your own organization. The method of identifying what needs to be benchmarked is to study your own business and try to work out which areas are suitable candidates for benchmarking. Sometimes such areas are pretty well known before you start, while in other cases it takes careful analysis of the business to narrow down and pinpoint the focus. However, it is your own organization and the people in it who largely determine the choice of subjects for analysis.

In addition, it is often necessary to look outside your own organization to identify areas suitable for benchmarking. You may thus need information from the market about your output of goods and services. How do customers rate the quality of your operations? A high volume of sales and good profitability may be the result of short-term profit maximization and are not necessarily good indicators of quality. You may also need to investigate what kinds of defects and mistakes occur, and how the pattern changes with time.

Deciding what to benchmark is largely a matter of knowing your own business. In benchmarking, therefore, you can take one substantial step towards success right from the start by making an analysis of what your organization does and what you want to benchmark. Define subactivities and functions as processes, and describe your operations in the form of a flowsheet. Creating a structural picture of your business, and thinking hard about what its inherent components are, can often give you an invaluable base on which to build your benchmarking programme.

To identify what to benchmark it is not enough simply to earmark certain areas for analysis. You also need to understand in depth the factors that influence the performance of the candidate for benchmarking. What critical factors in your business must be altered to get you into the world class? What are its critical performance factors? The meaning of the term performance factor varies according to what you are analyzing, as well as on the degree of resolution or depth of the analysis. You must be exactly aware of the critical performance factors of the area you are studying so that you can identify how excellence in these factors has been achieved by other businesses you are benchmarking.

As far as possible you should try to measure and compare critical performance factors in quantitative terms. The commonest way to measure performance is to express the result in revenues, costs and profitability. There are however other fine yardsticks as well, such as throughput time or quality parameters measured in units or percentages.

You must also decide how deep to make the benchmarking study. By depth we mean the level of resolution at which the comparisons will be made. The most usual practice is to benchmark at three levels of resolution, starting with the whole and then penetrating down into the organization in two stages. In a benchmarking project with the focus on productivity, the starting point may be to compare value-added productivity per employee. The next step is to break down the value-added term into its principal components, such as turnover, purchasing, personnel costs, overheads and capital costs, and express these for example as level of overheads per employee, personnel cost per pound of turnover, and so on. In the third step you can make a further breakdown of the business for in-depth understanding, and analyze such details as rental costs per employee.

If you are genuinely uncertain about what part or parts of the business ought to be benchmarked, you can start with the whole and work your way down step by step to identify "suspects", i.e. candidates for improvement. Using bench-marking for such exploratory purposes can be highly effective. Public-sector organizations and monopoly companies, in particular, may be truly ignorant of where the opportunities for improving their operations lie. Exploratory use of benchmarking is a fruitful method, especially in internal and external benchmarking, for identifying areas with a potential for improvement that need to be benchmarked further and areas that are performing relatively well compared to their equivalents elsewhere.

The first stage of the benchmarking process, deciding what to benchmark, thus includes the following items:

- What is the need and where does it exist in your organization?
- What do people outside your organization think of your performance?
- Know thyself! Survey your operations.
- If you do not know what area needs to be benchmarked, use the method to explore.
- Identify and learn the factors that are critical to performance and the units in which they can be measured.
- Decide on the appropriate level of resolution for the study.

Identify the Needs of Your Own Business

Benchmarking can be applied to all or part of a business and in many dimensions. The best approach depends on circumstances, and should be chosen in such a way as best to satisfy existing needs and accomplish your chosen purpose. The word *need* is of key importance as a starting point for selecting candidates for benchmarking. The needs of your own organization are always the prime criterion. If the study embraces the whole of your business, it is the needs of the whole that rule. If it is focussed on one aspect of your business, then the needs of the parts covered by the study determine what should be benchmarked. We can put it this way: there is always a customer whom the benchmarking project must satisfy.

The customer/client may be the chief executive of the company or organization itself, the collective management, the development department or line managers on various levels. The supplier of benchmarking is the project team appointed to do the job. The question of what to benchmark must therefore always be determined by the needs and requirements of the customer, and it is the duty of the project team to satisfy those needs. A common mistake is to try and do too many things at once, thereby running the risk that the study will be too thinly spread and will lack analytical incisiveness. On the other hand the terms of reference must not be so narrow as to put blinkers on the team, robbing it of perspective and the opportunity to propose far-reaching changes. Even a small-scale benchmarking project makes substantial demands on resources, but if the analysis meets requirements and lives up to expectations, it is always a good investment. If on the other hand the project is allowed to live its own life without being firmly linked to the client's needs, it risks turning out to be a rather expensive exercise.

The whole thing starts with an organization, company or individual with a stated need to make improvements with a view to being more efficient. There is a desire to develop and improve operations by learning from others without having to constantly reinvent the wheel. As we noted in an earlier chapter, one of the great strengths of benchmarking is that it can encourage market-type economics in operations whose true performance is otherwise difficult to assess. Support functions such as staffs and administrative departments are especially suitable candidates. So are functions which deliver to internal customers and are thus not exposed to market forces; benchmarking gives a measure of the quality and value which they actually deliver.

Devote time to workmanlike meetings for discussion of benchmarking areas with the responsible managers to narrow down the focus of analysis. What problems and factors underlie the need for change, and how can they be tackled? Let this be a creative process, a brainstorming session if you like, to avoid excluding ideas and suggestions that may later turn out to be strokes of genius. In some cases, however, this part of the project is much less dramatic because there is usually a fair degree of self-diagnostic insight about the relevant focus of benchmarking and where the potential for improvement lies. The actual reason for choosing benchmarking as a method may be that an area has been earmarked for comparison with internal or external leaders in its field. The area to be analyzed may also be known in advance or predetermined because the benchmarking study is a planned element in a larger revamping project with more than one dimension, and the needs of the organization are impelled by other factors than those of the benchmarking approach.

All aspects of an organization's behaviour and performance can be benchmarked: goods, services, processes, support systems, staffs, costs, capital, customer-perceived value, and so on. The applications, too, are many: such as new strategies, planning, cost reduction, focus on performance, new ideas, better quality.

How Do Others View Your Performance?

To further clarify the picture of your own performance, you can ask your customers what they think of it. Customer-perceived value is usually defined as the quotient between the quality of a product or service and its price. This is illustrated graphically in the value graph, Figure 23. If customer-perceived value lies within the shaded area, the quality variables of the product match the price that customers are willing to pay. The customer, in other words, regards the product or service as being worth the asking price. Price in this context usually means cash, but can also be some other sacrifice made for the sake of obtaining something desired.

THE VALUE GRAPH

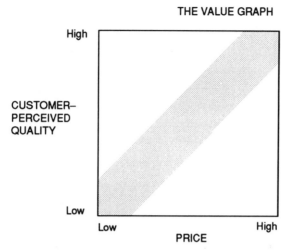

Figure 23 *The value graph illustrates customer-perceived value, which is a function of quality variables and price. If a product or service is in the top left-hand corner of the graph the customer feels he is getting his money's worth, whereas if it is in the bottom right-hand corner he does not think it is worth the price*

The vertical axis of the graph represents the quality variables of the product. It is a common mistake to identify variables solely in terms of concrete performance, such as whether a car has 4-wheel drive or whether a hotel room has cable TV; the term quality variables includes not only such concrete items but also abstract variables which are more difficult to quantify, such as service attributes and image (Figure 24).

For purposes of identifying areas for benchmarking analysis, you can investigate customers' perceptions of the value of what you deliver simply by asking a number of your largest or most important customers. Often, too, this knowledge is already available in the company in the form of market surveys, customer analyses and regularly updated customer barometers. Investigate what information already exists in-house before starting any new poll. It seldom requires an expensive large-scale exercise to discover customers' views; all it usually takes is a few telephone calls. If the subject of the benchmarking study is an internal department delivering to other internal departments, then the customers are right there under your own roof.

CUSTOMER - PERCEIVED QUALITY
(Harley Davidson Motorcycles)

PRODUCT ATTRIBUTES	SERVICE ATTRIBUTES	IMAGE
(Examples)	*(Examples)*	*(Examples)*
Performance Equipment	Spare parts Accessories	Ostentation Individualism

Figure 24 *The criteria of customer-perceived quality for a Harley Davidson motor cycle have other dimensions besides direct product attributes such as performance and equipment. These include for example after-market attributes such as spare parts and accessories and, no less important, image or prestige factors—the ability to attract attention and give the owner a feeling of fulfilment*

Try to form an appreciation of the following points:

1 How do customers perceive the quality of what your organization produces? Remember that the term quality is often only vaguely understood and does not mean the same thing to everybody. You can however get a fair idea of where you are if the answer is "excellent" or "unsatisfactory".
2 In the case of internal deliveries, you should try to assess the strength of demand for the product or service in question among those for whom it is intended. The number of internal monthly reports that are never read or analyzed, for example, is legion.
3 If the business serves more than one market and/or segment, you should try to distinguish between them if this can be done without a massive effort.
4 How well does the product or service work in practice? Identify faults or deficiencies that customers experience when the product is used for its intended purpose.
5 If possible, try to get some idea of how customers' perceptions of value have changed over a period of time—for better or worse. Can you identify any discontinuities in the curve attributable to external or internal events?

Information bearing on customer-perceived value can be gathered from several sources besides putting the question direct to the customer. Members of departments with a large interface with the market—sales, service, repairs—are one such source. Others include trade associations, independent reviewing bodies, and so on, who may have done some kind of market survey. You can also analyze indicators of various kinds such as frequency of complaints, guarantee claims, spare part consumption, repairs and level of discounts. All have the same purpose, to locate areas which have a potential for improvement and are thus candidates for benchmarking.

Figure 25 shows an example from heavy manufacturing industry; it can serve to illustrate a technique for identifying customer preferences. The company delivers machinery to the steel industry and has customers in 22 countries. The figure summarizes the relative importance of various aspects of performance. It compares customers' actual evaluations of the

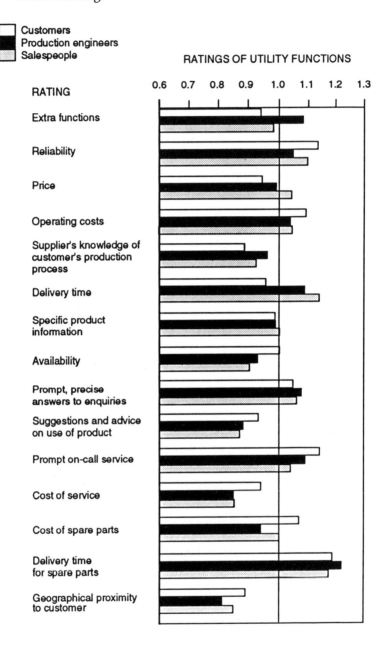

Figure 25   *The comparison shows that customers are not impressed by extra product functions (top), while production engineers think they are important. Customers, on the other hand, attach great importance to low spare part prices (3rd from bottom), while production engineers do not*

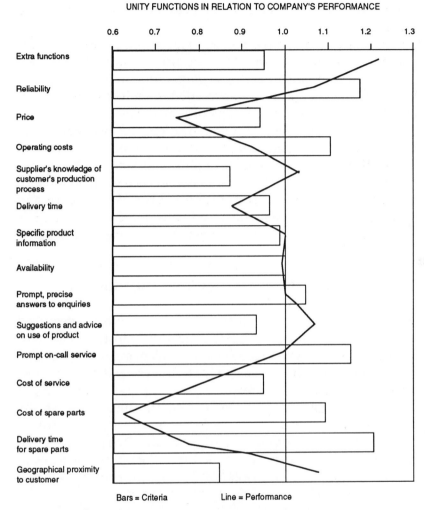

UNITY FUNCTIONS IN RELATION TO COMPANY'S PERFORMANCE

Bars = Criteria   Line = Performance

Figure 26 *The bars show customers' ratings of the importance of various performance criteria. The curve marks their ratings of the company's ability to satisfy the same criteria*

importance of each criterion (function, reliability, etc.) with what production engineers and salespeople think is important. Where an item is important to customers the score is greater than one; if it is unimportant, the score is less than one.

The figure reveals that customers' criteria of evaluation differ considerably from those of production engineers and salespeople.

There are also noticeable differences between the last two categories.

In the next stage of the survey (Figure 26), customers were asked to evaluate the company's performance according to each criterion in comparison with its competitors, to get a picture of how well the company had succeeded in delivering value that matched customers' weightings of performance criteria.

This survey revealed a wide discrepancy between what customers think is important and the company's ability to satisfy their demands. On the right-hand side of the figure, for example, we can see that customers attached great importance to after-market aspects (price of service, price of spare parts and speed of spare part deliveries), but considered the company's performance in these areas was inferior to that of its competitors.

Know Thyself! Survey Your Operations

An overall discussion and initial analysis of the kind just described is naturally not always enough to identify the most suitable areas for benchmarking with precision; the problem may call for a more structured approach. You may have to analyze and describe your business in somewhat greater detail to acquire the in-depth knowledge and insight you need to direct the focus of the study.

An excellent way to do so is to try and make a structured description of the component parts and operative processes that make up the business. Economic theory offers many ways of analyzing and describing organized activities. They all have the common aim of structuring and summarizing a business by generalization and simplification in order to make its inherent logic comprehensible. Perhaps the best-known recent example is the Value Chain model constructed by Harvard Professor Michael Porter (Figure 27). The Value Chain has existed for a long time, but it was Porter who popularized it. It is one of the first attempts in the field of strategy to penetrate and identify the structure of customer needs, utilizing the rational parts of a business to classify the structure according to the underlying activities of each part and the reason for which it exists.

Porter divides business into primary and support activities. The primary activities appear in the lower half of the figure: inward

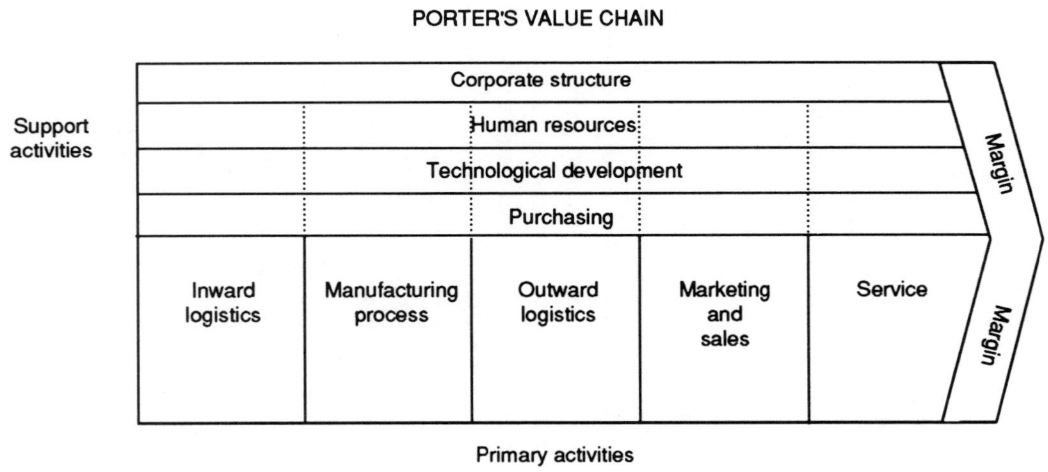

PORTER'S VALUE CHAIN

Figure 27 The American management professor Michael Porter, by centring his thinking around the Value Chain, has made a major contribution to its widespread use as a management concept

logistics, manufacturing, outward logistics, marketing and sales, and after-market service. These are supported by a number of infrastructural activities listed in the upper half of the figure.

The Value Chain is one option if you want to throw light upon the structure of your business in order to generate a basis of facts to help you identify benchmarking partners. Porter's version of the Value Chain is not the only possible one; several variations and simplifications of it are conceivable.

All this talk about the Value Chain may seem somewhat abstruse and perhaps irrelevant to practical problems. Using general models of this kind to describe a complicated reality may sometimes confuse more than it clarifies. But a description of the operative content of a business need not necessarily be complicated, as the example in Figure 28 illustrates.

The figure shows a simple but eminently practical method of breaking down the business of a painting firm into its principal activities. This model is the result of an external benchmarking project which compared three fairly large companies in the painting business. The aims of the project were to identify excellence in qualitative factors—satisfaction of customers' needs in terms of delivery precision and ability to meet buyers' specifications—and in productivity factors with the focus on possibilities for cost reduction. The project was run as an open comparison. To establish a structured framework of what was to be benchmarked, the business was broken down into the principal activities of which the logic of the painting trade is composed. The business can be divided into five component parts: management and administration, production control, material handling, tendering and production. The contents of the "boxes" and the boundaries between them consist of activity- and business-related factors, so the model describes the business from an activity-based standpoint. In addition, it cuts away activities which can be immediately recognized as non-comparable; thus it was decided that the painting goods shop which one of the companies operated should be excluded.

This example from the painting trade shows how the complete scope of a business and its component activities can be described. The model identifies those component parts which, together with the whole, are the focus of the benchmarking study. In this case the performance of the business as a whole was benchmarked,

Management, accounting and administration	Production control	Materials handling	Tendering	Production
* Staff (including management)	* Staff (including supervisors)	* Drivers	* Resource planning	* Personnel costs
* Premises	* Company cars	* Vehicles	* Costing	* Material purchasing
* Marketing	* Site preparation	* Equipment rental	* Reading & interpretation of documents	* Travel expenses
* Office overhead	* Follow-up: - documentation - work reports	* Returns and wastage	* Tender writing	* Service vans
* Other costs	* Miscellaneous		* Bookings	* Follow-up: - faults - deficiencies
			* Negotiations	
			* Brought-in costings	

Figure 28 This model is the result of a benchmarking study of the business as a whole and its component activities, which are represented by the five boxes

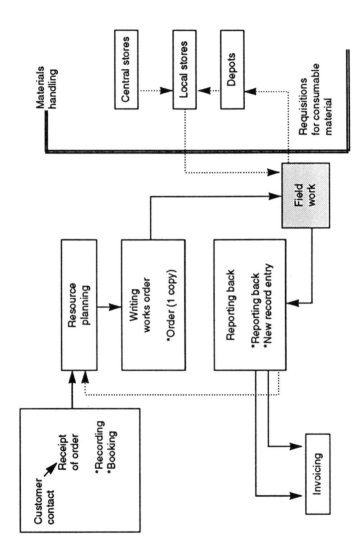

Figure 29 Flowsheet of operations from customer contact to invoicing for a service group which performs trouble-shooting and guarantee service on personal computers

and so were all the individual "boxes". Operations in the production control box, for example, were compared and analyzed with reference to precision of deliveries to work in progress, ability to manage production in compliance with quality norms specified in quotations, and cost per man-hour.

Another very useful way to describe a business is to start with operative processes and describe the flows which they generate. The next example (Figure 29) illustrates work flows in a service unit of a global data processing (personal computer) company. This department of the company provides trouble-shooting and guarantee service in a defined geographical area. To live up to the company's overall philosophy of quality, it operates a policy of correcting all faults within four hours. To be able to do so without incurring unmanageably high costs, it must have a smooth-running system for resource management. However, the department had trouble meeting its service commitments, so it decided to run a benchmarking project to find outstanding companies who had solved the problem.

To identify the detailed structure of the business and analyze the location of problem spots, operations are mapped in the form of a flowsheet. This describes the flow of events from when a customer phones in an order until the job is invoiced.

Once the business has been mapped, problems and bottlenecks can be identified. In the case illustrated here, three areas were identified as critical and thus as subjects for benchmarking:

1 Discrepancy between information available to the order-processing section and customer's actual situation.
2 Difficulty of optimizing stock-keeping when the number of stock points exceeds 65 000.
3 Long elapsed time between completion of work and invoicing.

Exploratory Benchmarking

A preparatory analysis is not always sufficient or even appropriate as a way to identify areas with potential for improvement. But benchmarking can be used for exploratory or diagnostic purposes to locate the areas where improvements are possible. By starting with the whole and breaking it down into its hierarchic pieces, you can perform a multistage benchmarking operation.

Large corporations and organizations contain numerous functions and subfunctions isolated from anything resembling market forces; they make only internal deliveries and have no idea at all of how their performance compares in efficiency with the situation in the outside world. We very often find, especially in the public sector, units that live by push of supply rather than pull of demand. These units may be highly productive, delivering large volumes of output, without ever asking themselves whether there is any real demand for what they produce.

So let the benchmarking study proceed from the whole and explore the parts to find the places which will be the subjects of deeper benchmarking analyses. The initial phase, when the whole and its component parts are analyzed, need not focus so

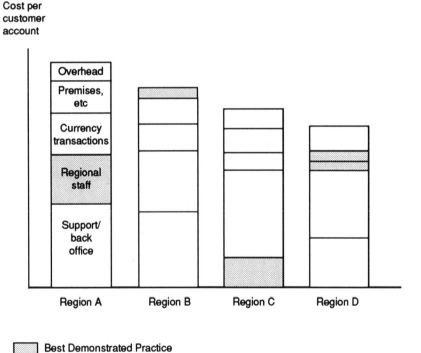

Figure 30 A graphic representation of an exploratory benchmarking study among the regional branches of a national bank. Although Region D has the lowest overall cost per customer account, there is room for improvement in parts of its operations. The shaded areas show lowest cost per account for specific items

sharply on underlying operative content; its primary purpose is to assess the situation and earmark interesting and suitable areas for in-depth benchmarking. The exploratory benchmarking exercise is in the nature of a "rough and ready" study. Using benchmarking in this way also gives an impression of the overall performance of the organization.

Figure 30 is an example of how exploratory benchmarking of a whole organization and its parts can identify areas in need of improvement as well as others that are performing relatively well. A regional manager of a national bank was certainly happy to represent the region with the best overall record (Region D in the figure). The result, expressed in cost per customer account, was measured by the bottom line of the profit-and-loss account.

But the question, "What is the weakest link in your operations?" was not so easy to answer. Internal benchmarking nevertheless revealed considerable potential for improvement by breaking down the whole business into its functional components. Although one region showed the best overall result, it could still improve its cost-per-account productivity by adopting the best practices from equivalent subfunctions in other regions; the manager of Region D had a lot to learn from Region A about rational personnel planning, and from Region C about the back-office function. So to improve the performance of his region, he decided to proceed with benchmarking studies of those areas.

Identify and Learn the Factors that are Critical to Performance and How to Measure Them

Tracking down and identifying the areas to hit with benchmarking with reference to all or parts of a "champion" organization is of course an important step in deciding what to benchmark. But the next step, perhaps the most important of all, is that of carefully identifying and understanding which factors are critical to achieving excellence in the benchmarked function.

The processes, systems, achievements, and other points which account for the performance of an organization are designated critical performance factors. They are the instruments, the control levers, that can be manipulated to improve performance.

Understanding the Operative Content of Your Business

Benchmarking, as we have said, focusses strongly on performance in operative content. To be able to make meaningful comparisons with other organizations with a view to adopting what are identified as Best Demonstrated Practices, you must understand the processes, systems, achievements, and other points which explain the performance that gives top results.

However, performance factors are not nearly so hard to recognize as the above remarks may seem to imply. By far the most common units of performance in the business world are monetary units measuring revenues and costs. The profitability of a company expresses the performance which it aims at attaining as cheaply as possible. In benchmarking, however, these units are generally too coarse and imprecise. It is obviously not feasible to benchmark your own performance against that of the world's most profitable company and draw conclusions from that gross comparison about how you can achieve similar excellence. To be meaningful and successful, benchmarking must break the business down into a number of significant components.

You can use the following checklist of questions as an aid to recognizing the critical performance factors of your business. The original source was Rank Xerox's internal benchmarking programme, but over the years the list has been refined and improved. The questions, as we see, are of a fairly general nature; this means that not all of them are relevant in all situations. Use them as a guide, and test them on your organization.

1 Does the problem have to do with customer-perceived value or productivity?
2 What is the current output of the organization (or the part of it in question)? How is output measured?
3 What factors are important in terms of customer-perceived value? How is such value defined and measured?
4 What factors/functions/processes generate the most problems? Have the problems increased or diminished lately?
5 Are there areas where market forces do not operate?
6 What area or operation accounts for the largest share of total costs?

7 What problems are known and have been identified in the organization (or the part of it in question)? Have previous efforts been made to solve them?

8 What areas are shown by analysis of the business to hold the greatest potential for improvement?

9 What areas are critical to gaining a competitive edge?

10 Are the problems operative (short time scale, crisis) or strategic (long time scale, change of course)?

The nature of the operations to be performed, and by the same token the underlying factors that can assure success in performing them, naturally vary according to the level of resolution you are using. The most usual practice, as we said before, is to break the analysis down into three levels. You start with an aggregated whole, which may be the entire organization or a designated function thereof, and then break down operations in two further stages to reach the level where you can identify and understand the underlying performance factors.

Performance Factors and Units of Measurement

When looking for suitable units of measurement you should try to find units that are already in use in the organization, as these are readily available and are already known and recognized. The measurements used for benchmarking should be few, yet give a true reflection of performance. Which units you choose will depend largely on prevailing circumstances.

The most relevant performance factors vary according to whether the benchmarking analysis is focussed on quality or productivity or a combination of both. Benchmarking of both quality and productivity factors has been discussed earlier in this book.

What you need to do, then, is to understand and identify the relationships between the parts of the organization to be benchmarked, i.e. their structural makeup, how they are linked to the critical performance factors, and how you can measure performance. To make these relationships clearer you can construct a simple matrix as in Figure 31. The operations or subfunctions which form the focus of the analysis are listed in

FOCUS	PERFORMANCE	UNITS OF MEASUREMENT
(Example) Works orders	*(Example)* Support system for works orders	*(Example)* * Manual corrections (%) * Extra time involved by work on faulty instructions (%)

Figure 31 Rational handling of works orders calls for a smooth-running support system. If this system works as it should, the number of manual corrections that needs to be made will be minimized and the cost per run will be low

the left-hand column. In the second column you enter the critical performance factors which you have identified in consultation with the people directly involved. In the right-hand column you enter the units of measurement which most closely reflect performance. The example in the figure refers to installation operations in the telecommunications industry.

In this example, work specifications have been identified as a benchmarking area. The organization acts as a subcontractor, installing systems according to works orders received from the main contractor. These orders specify pre-planning, project engineering, and so on in detail. How well the instructions match conditions at the actual workplace is thus a critical factor. Errors in drawings or material specifications, for example, mean a lot of extra work for the subcontractor, leading to delays, deterioration of quality and higher installation costs.

This makes works orders a critical performance factor. The yardsticks of performance are thus the number of faulty orders that have to be corrected and the number of man-hours spent correcting faults, both measured as percentages of the total. The benchmarking exercise in this case aimed at identifying world class or Best Demonstrated Practice with reference to accuracy of works orders and the number of man-hours spent on them in order to find a standard of comparison. It is of course also essential to learn *how* the organization with the Best Demonstrated Practice operates, i.e. to understand and be able to explain why it performs better with regard to the critical factors.

The structural sequence focus–performance–measure of performance is also applicable to more complex relationships. Figure 32 describes this sequence with reference to a high-tech R&D company in the defence industry. This company develops large and extremely complex tactical command systems. It operates on a project basis, and the projects are extremely complex, with a normal lead time of three to five years. Critical performance factors and measurements of performance for this company are listed in the table; they were obtained by functional benchmarking of project management in R&D companies in other industries.

The table shows the "generic" performance factors which are critical to success in running large, long-term projects. The term generic here refers to factors which are not specific to one industry; the object is to find performance factors and measurements applicable to any kind of project work. The factors and measurements listed were obtained by in-depth interviews with people from the organization itself and with customers' representatives.

FOCUS	PERFORMANCE	UNITS OF MEASUREMENT
Project work in an R&D company	Specifications of requirements	Customer-perceived quality Costs Lead times
	Project planning	Costs Time Number of revisions
	Goal management	Deviation from checkpoints
	Deviation	Compliance with specifications
	Component synergy	Frequency of re-use
	Project budgeting	Cost accounting Follow-up

Figure 32 *Critical performance factors are not always "hard" ones like specifications of requirements and project budgets. Some are more difficult to measure, like goal management and deviation from specifications*

Use Quantitative Measurements

Comparisons should, as far as possible, be made in some kind of quantitative terms. Even when you are comparing the quality of work processes, for example, you should try to identify quantitative units of measurement that reflect quality. Descriptive comparisons can of course also be made to round out the picture, but in the absence of hard performance figures the result of a benchmarking study will be difficult to interpret and useful only as a talking point rather than a genuine fact-based input for implementing the performance identified as Best Demonstrated Practice.

The table in Figure 33 lists a large number of performance factors. It first appeared in *The Benchmarking Book* by Michael J. Spendolini (1992). The list is based on summaries of interviews with a large number of North American companies to determine what critical performance factors they used in their own benchmarking processes. It can serve as a collection of examples, but makes no claim whatsoever to be exhaustive.

What Level of Resolution Should the Study Aim For?

By level of resolution we mean depth of analysis. The level of resolution you choose will depend on what you are studying and, of course, on the time and resources you have at your disposal. One of the great arts of analytical investigation is that of combining divergence, i.e. breaking down elements of knowledge into their component parts, with convergence, i.e. extracting central conclusions from a number of defined elements of knowledge. Deciding on the right level of resolution for the task in hand is an art in itself, and calls for due deliberation.

The most common practice in benchmarking, we have found, is to use three levels of resolution. The first is a comparison on the aggregate level, after which the component parts are broken down in two further stages. The following series of bar charts (Figures 34–37) can serve as an illustration. They refer to an example of benchmarking in a business whose performance is largely defined in terms of the number of man-hours it can charge out to its customers with sustained norm-related quality of

MEASUREMENT OF PERFORMANCE
Examples from American benchmarking companies

CRITERIA OF PERFORMANCE	UNITS OF MEASUREMENT
Market share	Units Dollars
Profitability	Margin contribution Return on total capital or equity
Competitors' growth	Market share per segment
Materials	Proportion of total cost Price/volume Freight costs
Direct/indirect personnel costs	Proportion of total cost Number of employees per function Fixed/variable salary share including travel expenses, etc. Productive hours per employee Personnel profile
Capital costs	Rate of turnover: - total assets - fixed assets - inventory Depreciation policy Leasing costs Receivable from customers/due to suppliers
Product characteristics	Price strategy
Output performance	Per utility function
Service	Response time Average time of service call Order processing routines Production planning
Image	Customer awareness Intensity and cost of marketing Customer reactions to marketing campaigns, etc.

Figure 33

delivery. The benchmarking approach here was to identify how outstanding companies combine a level of quality that lives up to customers' expectations with the ability to produce customer-perceived value at a low cost. The example, which is

HOURLY COSTS

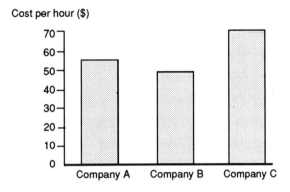

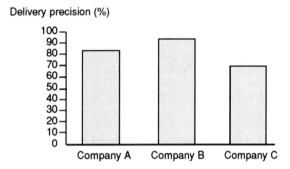

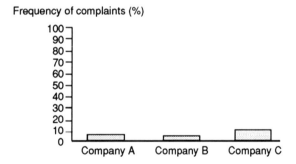

Figure 34 *Production costs per man-hour billed are compared for the whole business and for two quality variables: delivery precision (time) and complaints. To simplify the example, we assume that all companies in the comparison maintain norm-related quality standards; the intention is simply to illustrate different levels of resolution. To discover how one company differs from another in productivity, we analyze the business at two further levels*

HOURLY COST

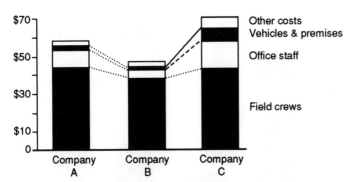

Figure 35 *This figure shows schematically how the analysis distinguishes between time-charging field crews, office staff, vehicles and premises, and other costs. At the next level these items are broken down into their components to get an in-depth picture of performance*

HOURLY COST FOR FIELD CREWS

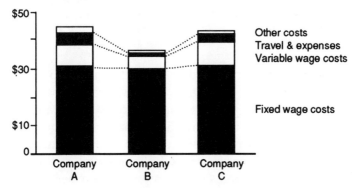

Figure 36 *The next step shows hourly costs for the field installation crews whose hours are billed to the customer. To analyze the business thoroughly and identify cost components, these items are broken down one step further*

considered strictly from the standpoint of productivity, demonstrates schematically how an operation can be broken down analytically.

Before You Go On

The first stage of a benchmarking process, deciding what to benchmark, comprises a review of your own organization's needs

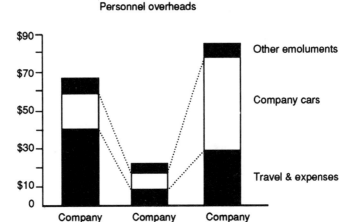

FIELD CREWS
Personnel overheads

Figure 37 At the finest level of resolution, the expenses of time-charged personnel are compared. The next step is to analyze the underlying operative content to find out why Company B has the highest cost productivity of the three. How does this company manage to keep its production costs so low while still maintaining the same high norm-related quality as the others? What lessons can they apply to their own operations? Are there any factors that are not comparable?

and of the attitudes and needs of its customers. To clarify the picture so that you can narrow down the focus of your benchmarking study, you may also want to make a structural model of your operations in the form of a value chain or flowsheet. Another way to determine the focus of benchmarking is to start with the business as a whole and explore it to try and discover what area or areas could improve their performance in relation to that of comparable operations elsewhere. A final part of the work in the first stage is to identify and understand the critical performance factors of your operations and how they can be measured. Having done all that, you can start thinking about the question of where to locate the outstanding organizations that represent Best Demonstrated Practice.

5
Stage 2: Identify Benchmarking Partners

STAGE 2

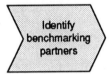

Figure 38

The purpose of the second stage is to identify, and establish relations with, companies and organizations whom you recognize as "world champions" in the areas in which you want to compare your own performance. By calling them benchmarking partners we emphasize that your relationship with them should be one of open exchange of information—not industrial espionage or anything of that nature. On the contrary, what you need is an interface that will enable you to set up and develop a long-lasting benchmarking collaboration.

Under certain conditions it may be fairly easy to locate external organizations that represent excellence. There may be experience and knowledge in your own organization that can point to companies who fulfil the requirements of a benchmarking partner. News media and published reports can also give you a fairly good idea of which companies or organizations would make good benchmarking partners. In other cases, however, the search for excellence may involve a systematic review of various types of business and industry.

Once you have identified a number of potential candidates, it is time to approach them and make contact. Establishing a relationship of mutual trust with a potential benchmarking partner usually calls for considerable thought and planning. In particular, if the company or organization you have in mind is located in a different part of the world with a different business culture and different customs, you must do your homework and prepare your approach carefully to maximize your chances of success. Our general experience, however, clearly confirms that companies and organizations which represent the Best Demonstrated Practice in their fields are far more willing to share their experience than one might initially suppose. The traditional Swedish bias towards monopoly and oligopoly, for example, is nowadays giving way to a far more performance-oriented attitude and a greater willingness to communicate with the outside world. Benchmarking can thus be seen as one of a number of important instruments for the promotion of global competitiveness.

The title of the book by Tom Peters and Robert Waterman, *In Search of Excellence* (1982), can very well double as the headline for the part of the process that deals with finding and identifying the companies and organizations that represent excellence. The objects of the search are businesses, functional units or outputs which are the best of their kind, or even best in the world. The whole point of the exercise is to learn from others the processes and methods, or parts thereof, that hold the key to greater efficiency expressed as higher customer-perceived value, or to lower production costs expressed as higher productivity. So why aim for the treetops when the stars are within reach? By stars we mean the companies and organizations that represent the very best, the ones whose very existence proves that what they have done really can be done, and is not just an ideal but unrealistic dream. The problem is to find the stars and find out how they manage to shine in a not always cloudless sky.

The second stage of the benchmarking process, identifying benchmarking partners, comprises the following steps:

- *Decision* on whether to run the study internally, within your organization, or to compare yourself with others outside it.
- *Search* to find the companies that represent Best Demonstrated Practice.
- *Contact* with benchmarking partners to secure their acceptance and collaboration.

Internal, External or Functional Benchmarking?

How you pursue your search for excellence depends on what you hope to achieve and how high you have set your sights (Figure 39). If your aim is simply to be "top of the class" in your own sphere by making an internal comparison with similar operations, e.g. in regions or subsidiaries, then all you have to do is convince your colleagues within your own group of companies. If on the

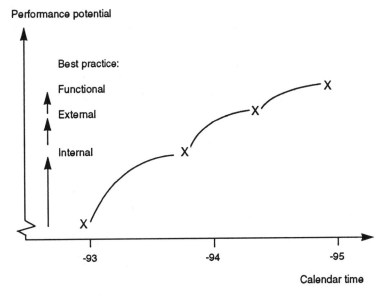

Figure 39 *Functional benchmarking offers the greatest potential for finding major improvements. However, as the figure shows, considerable opportunities for improvement can also be found through internal and external benchmarking. It is often a good plan to start with internal benchmarking, if points of comparison can be found within the organization, and then go on to external and functional benchmarking*

other hand you are interested in what your competitors are doing or if you have opposite numbers in other countries with a high degree of comparability, then your horizon will be an external comparison. And if you are looking for world-class excellence regardless of type of business, then you can search without limit. In this last case you will normally only be able to benchmark parts of your operations, but on the other hand the potential for success is very high. Please refer back to Chapter 2 for a more detailed presentation of the three categories of benchmarking.

There is really no exact decision point at which you opt for internal, external or functional benchmarking. If your own organization lacks any kind of branch structure, the choice is a simple one. But if you have to decide between internal and external benchmarking, the situation is different. Our advice in most cases would be that internal benchmarking is preferable as a first step in learning how to use the benchmarking method.

An opinion about whether to opt for internal or external benchmarking usually forms itself fairly early in the proceedings, so that when the time comes to pick a benchmarking partner the question is already settled in practice. You can very well decide right from the start to combine internal and external benchmarking, simultaneously comparing a number of internal operations in your branch structure with similar operations that you have identified in other organizations (Figure 40).

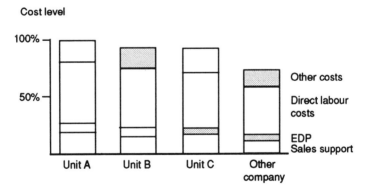

Figure 40 *The figure exemplifies a combination of internal and external benchmarking with reference to sales productivity in an industrial robot dealership. All regions of the company were included in the benchmarking study together with another company competing in the same type of business (right-hand column)*

Internal Benchmarking

When top management has given its blessing to an internal benchmarking project, getting hold of the data and information you need is normally less of a problem than if you have to research them from outside sources. Beware, however, of underestimating the problem of comparability. Internal, decentralized units which look very much alike in organizational terms on paper may in fact differ considerably in their underlying operative processes and even in their information systems.

Even in internal benchmarking, however, the chances of success are high. Even though you probably cannot count on finding world-class excellence by an in-house search, such a search can nevertheless reveal promising possibilities for improvement. An internal benchmarking project, moreover, is a splendid way to educate people in the benchmarking method and to focus their attention on operative content and performance.

External Benchmarking

The term external benchmarking refers to comparisons with competitors, i.e. with players offering the same kind of output, or a substitute that satisfies the same needs, to the same market. It may also include producers of the same kind of output who are not in direct competition with each other, such as national civil aviation and postal authorities or tourist resorts with different catchment areas.

Identifying competitors who are interesting from the point of view of benchmarking is not as simple or easy as it might appear at first sight. The competitor who is most profitable according to the "bottom line" is not necessarily the one who is the best performer in the particular areas you have chosen to benchmark. It also requires a good deal of systematic preparation to devise the best way to approach your competitor and convince him that your intentions are strictly honourable, i.e. that what you are proposing will be mutually beneficial. In the automotive industry they speak of "co-opetition", a hybrid between co-operation and competition. The basic idea behind it is to reconcile these two disparate concepts by using benchmarking to pool information and knowledge which benefit the industry as a whole from the standpoint of production, even while companies are fiercely competing with each other for the favour of customers.

In the case of businesses which supply the same kind of output to different markets, the chances of securing acceptance and co-operation are much greater. Here we often find a clear and explicit enthusiasm for benchmarking. Here, too, there are very real opportunities for setting up personal benchmarking networks that can be maintained for long periods of time. The current trend towards globalization and homogenization of business (especially in Europe through the EC) does however have the effect of expanding the markets served by individual businesses. In telecommunications, for example, where national authorities with a monopoly on their own ground were almost taken for granted until quite recently, the radical changes now in progress are creating new constellations and new competitive relationships.

Functional Benchmarking

Seeking world-class excellence, wherever it may be found, to apply to parts of one's own operations is of course the category of benchmarking that offers the greatest potential for effectiveness. Functional benchmarking can be regarded as a "nobler" form of external benchmarking in which comparisons are made between similar functions without regard to the type of industry within which they operate. There is no real limit to the field in which excellence may be sought; benchmarking partners may be spotted and identified almost anywhere. In functional benchmarking, the object of the search is the "champion of champions", and the difficulty lies in determining who the champions really are. But once you have done this, and made contact, there is seldom any difficulty in getting access to relevant information. Our experience is rather that recipients of benchmarking proposals are flattered at being singled out, and only too happy to share their knowledge and experience.

Where Can You Find Outstanding Companies?

The hunt for suitable benchmarking partners involves a systematic search of various sources of information, from the written records and personal experience available in your own organization to published reports and news media. Consultants and information specialists can also be a great help.

There are numerous methods and sources that you can use to gather information and guide the search for excellent benchmarking partners in the right direction. The price varies a great deal according to the method and source, from statistics and information that are available free of charge from official and other public sources to buying excerpts from databases or engaging the services of outside consultants. Several possible sources are listed and discussed below. You can try trade and employers' associations, commercial databases and published reports and statistics as well as in-house networks and knowledge. The search for one or more Best Demonstrated Practice organizations to compare yourself with often involves using more than one source of information. You may for example start by finding out what you can from your own internal networks and facts known to your organization to form hypotheses, and then try to verify the hypotheses by searching areas such as commercial databases and companies' annual reports.

Trade Associations

Most countries have a well-developed system of trade associations which exist to promote the collective interests of members of their industries. These associations are often very well informed about their member companies, and usually keep comprehensive statistics which, moreover, are available to any interested party. From a trade association you can get an overall picture of an industry in the form of various statistics and measurements. You can also, in some cases, get facts about specific companies—at the very least their addresses and telephone and fax numbers.

Databases

The growth of information technology has made databases a highly valuable and voluminous font of knowledge. Databases are available today with facts from an enormous variety of fields and with almost incredible coverage. Commercial databases are of two types, primary and secondary. Primary data means that all the information is collected *in toto*; these are also called fact or full-text databases, and they give you direct access to the data you are looking for. A secondary database tells you where to find the primary database that contains the information you want. In addition to references, a secondary database usually contains abstracts of original documents.

The knowledge you can access from a database is both varied and broad. You can search by keywords and, in principle, get out all written records and other documents in which the keyword appears.

Thus if you want to find a benchmarking partner who is a world-class performer in the area of just-in-time delivery, you can use JIT as a keyword to find what has been written and documented concerning that concept. If this in turn leads you to interesting articles in the trade and business press, you can often find references to outstanding companies who can be approached about a benchmarking partnership.

Several commercial databases also offer information service consultancy. In other words, you can get active help in finding the information you need. Commercial databases are available in most industrialized countries and are usually of excellent quality. Most universities and colleges of commerce also have their own databases, which can be very helpful.

Best Practice Databases

As a result of the successful emergence of benchmarking as a powerful instrument of change, several Best Practice databases have been established with a specific focus on benchmarking. These originated in the United States, on initiatives from various sources. The quality of their contents does not normally suffice for full-blown benchmarking, but they can be eminently suitable for finding overall points of comparison and identifying benchmarking partners. Several international accountancy firms, moreover, have their own Best Practice databases in which they have collected information about a large number of companies identified as outstanding in their respective fields. Here you can find facts about productivity as well as some measurements of quality and operative processes. However, we must issue a warning about placing too much faith in the quality of these databases. Information is a perishable commodity, and experience shows that it has proved difficult to keep this kind of high-quality data fully up to date. Nonetheless, Best Practice databases of this kind can be a splendid diagnostic aid to identifying benchmarking partners.

Published Reports and Statistics

Our modern Information Society produces large volumes of statistics and reports which can hold very useful clues to finding outstanding companies around the world. The OECD, for example, issues large numbers of extremely well-informed and interesting reports that spotlight and analyze various types of business and other activities. Some reports are of such outstanding quality that they directly provide information that can be used for comparative analysis. Other useful sources are the statistical yearbooks of various kinds that are published in most industrialized countries.

Company Networks and Organizations

Perhaps the most important and fruitful place of all to look for information about Best Demonstrated Practice companies is inside your own organization. People in product development and sales are usually very well informed about the industry they work in and where excellence is to be found within it; after all, they spend a large part of their time face to face with business development and competition from colleagues in the same line of business. So there is often a large fund of knowledge to be tapped in your own organization, and in our experience that is where you are most likely to find leads that will help you identify an outstanding benchmarking partner.

The help that you can get from your own organization in your search is not confined to information about your own industry. If you talk to department heads in your company, you will generally find that they know a lot about where excellence is to be found in their respective professional fields. If your intention is to benchmark efficiency in marketing, for example, and you ask your own marketing department where they think excellence is to be found, they will generally be able to cite cases from all kinds of industries. If you ask your financial director or controller who has the best and most advanced information and reporting systems, these specialists generally have a good idea of the situation in the business community at large.

Using your own organization as a base in your search for benchmarking partners opens up many more opportunities for creative searching. Thus if you want to benchmark delivery precision and customer service, you can ask your purchasing department to let you look at their records of dealings with suppliers. There is a good chance that those documents will show you a company with an excellent record that you would like to know more about. Moreover, you already have business relations with that company, which improves your prospects of gaining access to benchmarking data.

There are thus many ways in which you can seek information about companies and organizations to form an opinion about where to find excellence. The above list covers the five areas which we have found to be the most rewarding. But our most important experience, as we have mentioned, is that your own organization probably has a good "preconceived opinion" about where to look for excellence in the world around you. Advanced external research to identify Best Demonstrated Practice companies often fulfils the function of testing and modifying the hypotheses that you have already formed by polling the networks of your own organization. It is in specific functional benchmarking studies that the uncertainty factor is greatest and where it may take full-scale research to scan the world of business and administration for an outstanding partner.

The following table, while making no claim to be exhaustive, lists a number of sources where you can look for information:

Annual reports	Line colleagues
Board of Directors	Magazines
Commercial attachés	Management
Conferences	Market analysis department
Consultants	Marketing department
Corporate brochures	Product catalogues
Customers	Product development
Databases	Professional associations
Export councils	Purchasing department
House organs	Suppliers
Help wanted ads	Salespeople
Information firms	Trade associations
In-house databases	Trade centres
Internal sources	Trade fairs and exhibitions

No Benchmarking Partner Is Perfect

Good Example or World Class?

There is often a tendency among the benchmarking aristocracy to emphasize world-class standards. This is done whether you are talking about an important part of a corporation or a fairly minor function in need of direction for value creation and productivity, i.e. efficiency.

We have found it is counterproductive to look to examples which are way above as a benchmarking organization. We would therefore suggest that good examples should be found with the aim of creating sufficient improvement for the organization not to overreach itself, but to initiate change in terms of real improvement. If, at the end of the day, you might be in a position to reach world class, that is just fine. From the efficiency viewpoint, however, it makes more sense to lead the organization to what it has a chance of achieving rather than to what it could ultimately achieve in a distant future.

Let us therefore modify the extremely high ambitions of some of our American colleagues and recommend "sufficient" rather than maximum improvement. This does not imply any reduction of ambition. In our opinion it leads instead more rapidly and efficiently to the goal of continuous improvement. Once you have reached world class, there is nowhere else to go. The path to lasting improvement is one of continuous injections of energy and enjoyment.

Compromise

The search for benchmarking partners aims to find one or more who represent what can be regarded as top-class performance, and to establish a relationship that will enable you to identify and understand the performance that makes them so outstanding. Reality, however, is not all that simple. You may have to compromise to find an acceptable partner.

Your circumstances may differ to such an extent—though experience shows that this very seldom happens in practice—that no meaningful benchmarking comparison can be made. It may be found in international benchmarking, for example, that local conditions on another continent are of such a nature that what at first sight looked like world-class performance in a comparable field is the result of such special circumstances that there is a clear risk of the comparison being meaningless—like comparing apples and pears. In such cases you will have to look for a benchmarking partner whose circumstances more closely resemble your own.

Another compromise situation in which you may find yourself, and which may make your chosen partner unusable, however excellent he may be, is that he simply will not play; that he is not prepared to release benchmarking data to you. In some climates and some companies we sometimes find a technocratic cult of self-sufficiency that leads to that kind of behaviour. People are so proud of their success that they do not think it is desirable or necessary to learn anything from anybody else. This attitude, as we have said, is now on the decline, but in the choice between trying to benchmark "through the keyhole" or choosing the second-best partner, the latter option is usually preferable. The explanation may of course also be that your chosen partner is currently in the midst of a process of restructuring or other change and simply cannot spare the time or energy to get involved in a benchmarking relationship.

Establishing Contact with Benchmarking Partners

Having been involved in and responsible for a large number of benchmarking projects of varying scope and nature, we have noted that a certain diffidence and shyness set in when the time comes to approach the companies selected for partnership—especially when the method is being applied for the first time.

As long as people are in the familiar and comforting surroundings of their own offices, the project runs like clockwork. The project team works very hard at learning the new method, and the first step, analyzing and deciding what to benchmark, usually goes very well. The next step, looking around for companies or organizations to serve as objects of analysis, is not always easy but nevertheless normally assumes the aspect of a systematic process that presents no insurmountable difficulties. But when the time approaches actually to contact the companies identified as potential champions, the pace tends to slacken a little. It is a daunting prospect to introduce yourself and your business to people who may represent big corporations which are household names—and which, moreover, your own previous analysis has identified as "superior". So much greater, then, will be your joy in discovering how well things go once you have overcome your initial "stage fright", and how much friendly mutual curiosity the meeting soon generates. Shying from unaccustomed situations is not only a very human trait, but also a useful one in that it encourages extra thoroughness in preparing to take the plunge.

There are a couple of simple steps which, if followed, will smooth the approach to a prospective partner, so you should consider and prepare them carefully to maximize your chances of success.

1 Telephone or write a short letter stating what you have in mind and asking for an appointment for an initial meeting.

2 The initial meeting has two purposes:
  (a) to explain the project;
  (b) to supply the information that the other party needs in order
      to decide whether to agree.

The very first contact with a prospective partner has one purpose
only: to fix a date for an initial meeting. Do not try at this stage
to get a snap decision to participate in the project, unless the
other party makes the suggestion of his own accord. Draft a short
letter explaining in simple terms what you have in mind, and
address it to the management of the organization concerned.
Setting up an initial meeting with no strings attached does not
usually present any problems (except that of finding a time when
a number of busy executives are all free to come).

As noted above, an initial meeting with a prospective
benchmarking partner really only has two purposes. The first
is to propose and explain the project, and the second is to supply
the information the other party needs to make a decision about it.

Remember to emphasize that participation in a benchmarking
project also offers a number of benefits to the studied party. They
will gain knowledge and learning about other areas of business
in return for a very modest investment of resources. Although
they have been selected as representatives of excellence, it is still
highly probable that the study will give them new and useful
insights. In addition, their organization will get instruction in
the benchmarking method and practice in its application at no
extra cost—knowledge which they will then be able to apply in
future benchmarking projects of their own. Nor must we forget
the great human and professional bump of curiosity that can be
stimulated by the opportunity to learn about another
organization.

The agenda for the initial meeting should cover the following
items:

1 *Introduction of yourself and your company*
  You may be tempted to believe that the people you are visiting
  know all about your own organization, especially when you
  are making your pitch to a competitor or other company in
  the same line of business. Such belief is often unfounded, and
  you can win their trust right from the start with a well prepared

presentation of your business. Utilize this opportunity to tell them a little more than what they can read in your published annual reports. Tell them about interesting events and achievements that will reinforce their confidence in you as a person and prove that you are serious about your benchmarking proposal.

2 *Purpose and objectives of benchmarking*
Explain the general purpose and specific objectives of your benchmarking project, making it clear what the problem areas are and what you hope to accomplish. Do not assume that everybody present knows about benchmarking as a method of boosting efficiency, but describe the methodology. Explain, too, the ethics of benchmarking, under which one does not seek to acquire information about other organizations without being willing to divulge the same information about one's own.

3 *Project and action planning*
A detailed review of the project plan is not normally needed at this stage. In addition, it may be psychologically unwise to present a detailed "information shopping list" at the initial meeting without giving the other party a chance to influence its contents. There are however a few points you should mention: firstly you should indicate what type of information you are interested in, what measurements of performance you want to compare, what level of resolution you are aiming for, etc., and secondly you should give some idea of your proposed timetable.

4 *Reporting back*
A benchmarking partner is naturally entitled to receive a final report on the study once it has been made. The nature of this report will depend on how the project is conducted. In the case of a joint benchmarking project where the work is done by project groups in which all parties are represented, reports and project documentation will also be jointly produced. If on the other hand the emphasis is on one party benchmarking another, with perhaps several companies or organizations involved, then the data and analyses to be reported back should be agreed on in advance. The most usual, and recommended, practice is to deliver an anonymous, coded report where the benchmarked company is naturally informed of the codes that refer to its own operations.

Take No for an Answer

Almost inevitably, you will sooner or later be turned down by a prospective benchmarking partner. The company or organization concerned simply comes to the conclusion that it does not wish to participate. The reasons may be many and complicated, and you may not even be told why you are being turned down.

You must respect a rejection of your advances. It may be that the company concerned just does not have the time or ability, or is in the midst of a process of change that leaves no resources to spare for a benchmarking project.

Another reason for a negative reply to a benchmarking proposal may be that the object of your wooing is not in fact outstanding. Having heard your presentation of your company and your intentions, they may feel that they do not possess the excellence you have attributed to them. In such cases they will be apt to decline, often without telling you why.

To conclude our exposition of Stage 2, the identification of benchmarking partners, we wish once more to emphasize that the search for world-class performers calls for a large measure of creativity and imagination. You must widen your view and scan a broad spectrum of companies. You may find excellence where you least expect it.

6
Stage 3: Gather Information

STAGE 3

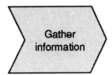

Figure 41

The purpose of the third stage, information gathering, is to supply the information needed for the analysis. It always starts in your own organization. There are two reasons for this. The first is that it teaches you a great deal about your business from the viewpoint and focus of what is to be benchmarked, and the second is that with your business as a frame of reference you can precisely define and specify what information you need, thereby increasing both the precision of your contacts with external partners and the quality of the data you get.

The very first thoughts about a benchmarking project usually revolve around the data-gathering phase. It is quite natural to assume that the need for information and knowledge about other people's excellence, alongside the need for change and improvement of your own operations, is central to the project. A "maiden" benchmarker often regards the collection of data as the vital and important part of the project, and believes that the success or failure of the work and analysis turns on this point.

The more experience of benchmarking you acquire, the more you will realize that the data-gathering phase is more a period of hard, purposeful work involving frequent contacts and working sessions with your benchmarking partners. Success depends more on how thoroughly you have planned and analyzed the scope of the work and chosen the subject for benchmarking, the method of measuring results and the benchmarking partner who represents the best possible example to follow.

This is not to say that the work of gathering data is uninteresting. Far from it! It is now that your view of your own organization's performance begins to clarify, with a series of new insights, while at the same time information on others' performance starts to flow in. This almost always spurs the project team to redouble their efforts.

The type and amount of information involved may vary widely. In benchmarking studies aiming at cost reduction, for example, you may have to cope with huge volumes of data from accounting and support systems to build up your fact base. On other projects, the amount of data may be much smaller. There is also considerable variation with regard to the number of sources from which data must be obtained. Sometimes all you need is the co-operation of a fairly small group of people who between them possess all the knowledge you need access to. Other cases call for numerous interactions with sources both inside and outside the business you are studying. People with relevant information to contribute to benchmarking may be found in various positions in the organization. You may also have to supplement your body of collected data from independent outside sources, such as published statistics and reports or interviews with customers and suppliers. It is an important truth which cannot be repeated too often that a small quantity of really reliable information is always preferable to a vast mass of information of dubious quality.

The third stage of benchmarking, information gathering, comprises the following main steps:

- Draw up questionnaires, including definitions and explanations where necessary.
- Collect information and compile data about your own business.
- Collect information from your benchmarking partner.
- Collect information from other sources.

- Document the information.
- Check and verify the information to ensure that it is fully approved by responsible managers in both your own organization and that of your benchmarking partner.

Draw Up Questionnaires

There are several advantages to starting the process of information gathering by preparing well-organized questionnaires. In the first place they give you an automatic framework for all the documentation you are going to have to compile, sort and organize. In the second place, this step offers a splendid opportunity to get the benchmarking study accepted by heads of profit centres by involving them in the task of specifying what information needs to be obtained.

In the first stage, deciding what to benchmark, you analyzed your own operations with reference to critical performance factors and the most appropriate units in which to measure them. Now you must consider in greater detail what kind of data and information you need to collect in order to understand and document the elements of performance. It will often also be necessary to spend time writing clear, simple definitions of the information content you are seeking in order to avoid misunderstandings and enhance comparability for purposes of analysis.

The quantity and complexity of the information you need will naturally vary considerably according to the nature and scope of the project. Our advice to draw up questionnaires and carefully specify their contents may seem too pedantic in cases where the scope is fairly modest and/or the nature of the information is not particularly complicated. Of course you should not over-analyze or over-bureaucratize the project by loading the questionnaire with definitions and specifications that are not essential to the task of benchmarking. Nevertheless, we urge thoroughness in preparing the information-gathering process as outlined. One seldom finds that a project review or follow-up of a benchmarking study comes to the conclusion that the project was over-planned and could have been completed with considerably less preparation.

You must also bear in mind that the information and data you gather in are almost always "living" material. However well you have prepared and tested your questions, the data-gathering process will always unearth new knowledge; this makes it difficult, well-nigh impossible, to formulate questionnaires in advance which will not have to be revised or clarified in some respect. If the body of information is large or complex, our experience shows that this type of preparation and planning is essential.

The questionnaire can be regarded as the measuring instrument of the study. A measuring instrument must satisfy a number of general criteria if its readings are to be trusted. It must measure what it is intended to measure, and not something else; we call this criterion *validity*. It must also give accurate readings, to satisfy the criterion of *reliability*.

You can clarify the aspect of validity by asking yourself what information is important and relevant for the purpose of identifying and measuring the critical performance factor concerned. If you are running an internal benchmarking project focussed on productivity per employee in a sales organization with several regional divisions, you may very well find that the general level of salaries is higher in metropolitan than in provincial regions. This phenomenon is caused not by differences in bonus earnings and similar incentives but by the fact that salaries have been inflated by competition for qualified personnel. If you fail to take account of this, your analysis will be biased against the metropolitan regions where salaries are higher.

A measuring instrument is said to be reliable if it yields the same result every time it measures the same factor or variable. If you have not defined and explained what you want to measure, or failed to make your intentions clear in other respects, you will risk getting different answers to the detriment of precision in your analysis. If for example your benchmarking study calls for information about the number of employees in a department, and you have not clearly defined what you mean by the term *employee*, you are likely to get different answers depending on whom you ask. If you ask the personnel manager, his answer will probably give you the total number of people on the payroll, regardless of whether they work full-time or part-time. But if you put the same question to a controller in the accounting department, his answer is likely to be expressed in full-time equivalents. This will undermine the reliability of the study.

Try to simplify as far as possible, giving clear limits and definitions of what you want to find out. Enlist the help of knowledgeable people in your own organization; this is often a very good way to increase both reliability and validity. Where such people are included in the project team, so much the better; otherwise you must search the organization to find them. Discuss and verify what kind of information you are after. Try to make interview checklists and questionnaires follow a logical sequence, beginning with general questions to establish an overall view and then proceeding to progressively more detailed questions.

There are five main types of questions you can ask:

1 Open questions.
2 Yes-or-no questions.
3 Multiple choice questions.
4 Scoring questions.
5 Data points.

1 *Open questions* are general ones with no preset answers to choose from or items to evaluate.
  Examples: What were your grounds for choosing the support system for your sales organization? How do you measure the quality of the operative content of your organization? What are your routines for dealing with faults reported by customers?
2 *Yes-or-no questions* give the respondent a simple choice of answering in the affirmative or negative. They may be followed up with a supplementary open question.
  Example: Have you a system for continuous measurement of customer satisfaction? (Yes/No)
  If Yes, can you describe its salient features?
  If No, why not?
3 *Multiple-choice questions* require the respondent to pick one of a number of alternative answers.
  Example: Which was the most important consideration when you chose your order processing/stock-keeping/invoicing system?

  • Cost-effectiveness?
  • Precision of delivery?
  • Ease of retrieving statistics and monitoring performance?

4 *Scoring questions* require the respondent to evaluate or rank various items.
Example: How important is it to you to have your own cleaning staff rather than hire the service from a cleaning firm?

- Not important at all.
- Preferable, but not absolutely essential.
- Very important (partly for reasons of security).

5 *Data point questions* are quantified questions requiring an "absolute" answer.
Examples: How many people are employed in your corporate staff group? What is your turnover per product group? What percentage of your customer deliveries are made on time?

To assure the quality of answers to data point questions you must carefully define and explain the nature of the information you want to elicit. If your questions are not so defined, the answers are liable to vary from one respondent to another (see under *reliability* above).

A data point question may often be a follow-up to a question in one of the four preceding categories.
Example: What are your priority areas for personnel training and development? followed by the questions:
What is your annual budget per employee?
How many days' training does the average employee receive?

Start with Your Own Business

All information gathering in benchmarking must proceed from and begin with your own business. Identifying and understanding its performance and work processes is not only a strength but almost an essential for being able to analyze other businesses and appreciate their excellence and thus to improve the performance of your own.

The focus of the analysis, i.e. the candidate for benchmarking, was identified in the first stage; that process should already have supplied the project team with a fund of knowledge about their own operations. Now the time has come to refine and sharpen knowledge of your own business by starting to collect internal information. The advantages of this method of approach can be described in five points:

1 The first advantage is that you get a chance to test your benchmarking model. When the project has progressed to the point where you have prepared questionnaires and are ready to harvest information from your own organization, you have already completed a number of important tasks. By analyzing the needs of your business you have identified what you want to benchmark, and you have also identified the outside companies or organizations which represent the excellence and Best Demonstrated Practice with which you want to compare yourself. In addition, you have given careful thought to formulating the questions you want answered. You might say that you have constructed a model of how a benchmarking study ought to be run. Analyzing your own operations at the outset gives you a splendid opportunity to test this model before applying it externally. You may find that in some areas you have partly or wholly underestimated the problems connected with information gathering, such as definitions or the necessary degree of depth and penetration. If you have correctly illuminated and understood the operation you have chosen to benchmark, it may turn out that you need more data. Even the less dramatic discovery of a need to modify and fine-tune both the model and the questions may prove both useful and necessary.

2 The second advantage is that you can utilize the internal information-gathering process to sell the idea of benchmarking more persuasively to people in your own organization. For action to improve results, based on outside observations of excellence, will eventually be implemented in the very same places where you are now seeking information. By testing and getting internal feedback on both the benchmarking method as such and the content and focus of the current information and data-gathering exercise, you can help to clarify the picture and increase the likelihood that enthusiasm and support for applying the lessons of external excellence will spread throughout the organization.

3 The third advantage is that greater knowledge of your own operations also contributes to knowledge and realization of

what the organization must do to improve its performance. You can get suggestions and ideas based on identified weaknesses in the present setup.

4 The fourth argument for starting to gather information at home is that it gives you and your project team useful training before you make contact with your external benchmarking partners. It is the rule rather than the exception that when you contact and interview outstanding companies and organizations about their operations, they will ask in turn how the equivalent operations are handled in your organization. There is an obvious risk of losing your benchmarking partner's confidence if you have not done your homework on that point.

5 Earlier in this book we discussed at length the ability of the benchmarking method to focus the efforts of an organization on performance in operative content. The fifth argument for starting the information-gathering process internally is associated with that discussion. By quickly acquiring an in-depth appreciation of your own organization's level of performance, you can identify and understand the excellent performance of benchmarking partners more readily and with greater precision.

Gathering Information from Benchmarking Partners

By the time you start to gather information and data from outside benchmarking partners, you should have tested your model and questionnaires on your own organization and checked that they work. Before you start contacting people in your partner's organization, whether by mail, telephone, video conference or face-to-face interview, you must make sure that you are going after the right people. Check with your contact person for safety's sake. Ask for a list of the best people to answer questions on specific subjects, together with their job titles.

Direct-dialling extension numbers and fax numbers, if any, are also useful.

There now follows a review of various channels for gathering information and data. You should use whichever the members of the project team feel most comfortable and at home with. You should however try to arrange at least one face-to-face meeting with those who are judged to be key people in your bench-marking partner's organization, preferably in their own offices.

Telephone Interviews

The telephone has many advantages as an interviewer's tool, but the greatest advantage of all is indisputably its low cost. A telephone conversation is much cheaper than a personal visit. The advantage, of course, is that you do not have to pay travelling or hotel expenses, not to mention the inherent unproductivity of travel time.

You can make all calls from one place—preferably your own office, with all background material and other information at your fingertips. The telephone is a particularly valuable instrument for referring back to earlier interviews, clearing up points of uncertainty, and so on. Especially if the benchmarking project is international in scope, the cost of an efficient telephone meeting is only a tenth of what a personal meeting would cost.

Using the telephone as a tool is also subject to a number of drawbacks, the nature of which is complementary to the advantages. There is of course a great advantage inherent in being able to talk to someone face to face. It is much easier that way to catch moods and signals, and thereby enhance the quality of the information you get. A face-to-face meeting, moreover, gives you much better opportunities to establish a personal relationship from which you can benefit during a prolonged period of collaboration on benchmarking. It is often easier for the interviewee to explain and account for his answers to questions in a face-to-face interview. Experience confirms that a telephone interview yields a more staccato type of information, making it difficult to catch all the shades of meaning in the total picture.

Another slightly more serious but unfortunately very common problem with telephone interviews is the difficulty of getting hold of the person you want. It is true that telecommunications technology is advancing with incredible speed and that mobile telephones and bleepers are quite common nowadays. However, you cannot always count on the exchange operator knowing the mobile or bleeper number of the person you want to reach, or being prepared to disclose it. How easy or hard it is to reach a given individual depends largely on their company's internal corporate culture. In some companies executives inform the exchange as a matter of course where they are and how they can be reached at all times. Other cultures lack these routines, relying instead on message-taking with a promise to call back, and so on.

If you are using the telephone as an information-gathering instrument, there are a few points you should bear in mind:

1 Always start the interview by introducing yourself and explaining what your purpose is, why you are calling that particular person, and who gave you his or her name. Try to make your initial pitch both courteous and interesting.
2 If the interviewee is a key person in your benchmarking project, you should preferably not use the telephone at all.
3 Complex issues are difficult to resolve over the telephone, so telephone interviews should concentrate on short questions.
4 By all means use the telephone as a follow-up instrument *after* a face-to-face interview to check facts and put supplementary questions.
5 Give the interviewee a chance to prepare by mailing or faxing your list of questions in advance.
6 Be sure to document the conversation, either by taking notes or by putting it on tape.
7 Put your questions in a logical order that makes it easy for the interviewee to follow your thought processes. Start with general questions and work down to more specific ones.

Video Conferences

The beauty of video conferences as a medium for interviews and working meetings is that they give you a *sense* of physical presence without actually having to be in the same place. Many large international corporations have now installed their own permanent video conference facilities; in other cases the local telecom service can usually provide them.

As an information-gathering instrument, the video conference shares with the telephone the major advantage of cost-effectiveness while partly remedying the telephone's lack of physical and visual contact. If you want to interview somebody located on another continent, or if several people in different locations are to take part in the conference, this medium is far, far cheaper than a personal visit. In addition, it allows you to display documents, text and graphics as an aid to discussing complex questions which require detailed answers and deliberation. The authors can confirm by personal experience that video conferences can contribute to the success of benchmarking studies.

Another great advantage of the video conference is that it is very easy to document the interview or conference simply by recording the session on videotape, so that the interesting parts can be played back and analyzed at leisure.

Your chances of success with a video conference will increase if you bear the following points in mind:

1 Introduce yourself and your company, explain your mission, and make sure that the video conference gets off to a good start.
2 Brief the interviewee by sending a copy of the questionnaire. Complicated questions, in particular, call for advance documentation.
3 Draw up an agenda for the meeting and get it agreed in advance, to ensure as far as possible that the meeting achieves its purpose.
4 Remember that the cost of a video conference is measured by the time it takes. Try to use the time efficiently.
5 People who are not used to video conferences may stiffen up when they realize that they are "on camera". Act naturally and try to put them at their ease!
6 Use the video system to document the conference.

The video conference, too, has disadvantages which cannot be overlooked. The cost of hiring the conference equipment and establishing the link is still fairly high. With the present pressure of competition in the travel business, face-to-face meetings may still be cheaper if the distance is short or if meetings are frequent.

Another disadvantage is that video conference equipment is not available for rent everywhere or on all occasions. The equipment is normally permanently installed, and not portable. It is quite expensive to install a video conference setup in your own offices, owing to the high standard of quality and level of resolution needed to transmit a good enough image to enable showing of graphics, tables, charts, and so on. The quality of video conference links is still somewhat variable. However, there is an enormous amount of technical development going on in this field; the next generation will probably abandon video technology altogether in favour of transmission via regular telecommunication lines.

Interviews by Mail and Fax

There are many kinds of information and data that can conveniently be obtained by sending out questionnaires. Examples include questions about customer satisfaction, criteria for norm-related quality, definitions and descriptions of various operations, cost specifications of various kinds, and other numerical data such as numbers of employees.

Mail and fax interviews should be regarded only as a supplement to other media such as telephone, video conference or face-to-face interviews.

Mail and fax interviews, like telephone interviews, enjoy a cost advantage over both video conferences and face-to-face interviews. The cost level is comparable to that of a telephone interview, perhaps even less because the respondent supplies the answers and data unprompted. Another advantage of mail and fax interviews is that they can all be handled by one person, who thus has a good oversight of the whole information-gathering operation. Yet another advantage, compared for example to the telephone, is that it is easier to reach the right person. It can virtually be taken for granted that most people nowadays have access to a functioning mail and fax distribution system that makes sure they receive messages addressed to them.

A final advantage is that the respondent can reply to the questions at leisure and with due deliberation instead of having to produce snap answers in the course of an interview. He or she can consult sources and check and verify facts.

An obvious disadvantage of the mail/fax interview is that it can never be used as the sole medium for gathering information. If you want to interview people whose specialized knowledge is essential to your benchmarking project, you need to talk to them face to face or at the very least by video. Here, however, a mail or fax interview can serve to complement or amplify other media. The fact that the interviewer is not personally present, or on the other end of a telephone line, when the questions are answered means that a mail or fax interview can be much slower than other ways of getting information. Another disadvantage is that you cannot establish a dialogue about the questions; the answers come unqueried.

Properly used, however, mail and fax interviews can be an invaluable aid in benchmarking. The following points can usefully be borne in mind:

1 Use the mails or fax as a complement to telephone or face-to-face interviews. They can be used to lay the groundwork for an interview as well as to collect supplementary and explanatory data afterwards.
2 Take care to get the interviewee's address or fax number right.
3 Follow up all mailings and fax messages with a phone call a day or two after the estimated time of delivery.
4 Add a paragraph in which you explain what your purpose is and who you and your company are.
5 Remember the security aspect. If the data you are asking for are critical or important, you should consider sending letters by registered mail or other secure means, especially to addressees in other countries.
6 Present the questions in a logical, comprehensible order to make them as easy to answer as possible.
7 If you send a letter, enclose a stamped self-addressed envelope.

Face-to-Face Interviews

The most interesting and in practice most effective method of acquiring information for benchmarking is to call on your benchmarking partner at his office and conduct a face-to-face interview there. This also gives you a chance to get acquainted with the atmosphere and environment in which your partner lives and moves and has his being. You can tour the premises and see with your own eyes what kind of methods and processes are being used. You can witness demonstrations of support systems and administrative aids, learn more about the goods and services the business produces, and take the opportunity to discuss pros and cons with the people on the spot.

The usefulness and success of a study visit to a benchmarking partner depend on the thoroughness with which it is prepared and planned. You must be aware that you are taking up the working time of busy professional people, so as a sheer matter of courtesy you should come well prepared. Your benchmarking partner's representatives must not be made to feel that the meeting was unbusinesslike and that the time could have been better spent on other things. This does not mean that you should rush through the meeting in the shortest possible time, which will only undermine the quality of the information and data you get out of it; what it means is that the operative time set aside for meetings and interviews should be effectively utilized, with the help of proper planning, to acquire a maximum of useful information and data.

An interview visit to a benchmarking partner is conditional upon the idea of a benchmarking study having been proposed and accepted (see *Stage 2: Identify Benchmarking Partners*). If a working meeting has been arranged with somebody who, despite the preparations, has not been directly informed about the project, be prepared to give a short rundown on the background to the project, why it has been started and what it is intended to accomplish. This is important, especially with a view to putting the interviewee at ease and engaging his interest in the project. There is also the risk that the quality of the answers will suffer if the respondent is not fully aware of why the questions are being asked.

As we have said, personal visits and interviews have both advantages and drawbacks. The quality of the information is usually much better than what you can get from either mail, fax, telephone or video conference interviews. The major disadvantage of a face-to-face interview is of course the cost it entails. Even visits inside your own country can involve not only travelling expenses but also overnight stays with board, lodging and subsistence on the expense sheet. Nevertheless, the very real advantages of a face-to-face interview make it highly advisable to have at least *one* such interview with each benchmarking partner, cost what it may. Once you have established personal contact the other media—mail, fax, telephone and video conference—become much more effective instruments for follow-up and fine-tuning in the data-gathering process.

We repeat: the success of a personal visit to and interview with a benchmarking partner depends on the thoroughness with which it is prepared. Here is a checklist of points to remember:

1 It is essential to start off on the right foot. Begin by introducing yourself and your company and briefly explaining your mission. Try to strike a friendly but businesslike note.

2 Make sure that you meet the right person, i.e. the one best qualified to inform you about the excellence of your benchmarking partner.

3 Confirm the time and place of the meeting (including the time it is scheduled to end) in writing to avoid any misunderstanding.

4 Send the interviewee a letter or fax message containing a brief rundown on yourself, your company and your mission, as well as the questions and questionnaires you plan to submit. If the questions are of a complicated nature, it may be best just to send a brief advance summary of the areas you want to cover and to bring the specific questions with you to the meeting—again to avoid any misunderstandings.

5 Do not expect one meeting to supply all the information and data you need. If you are pressed for time, take up the overall and complex questions while you are there and follow up by telephone, mail or fax to get the specifics.

6 Do your homework as thoroughly as possible by reading annual reports and any other published information you can get hold of.

7 Be ready for counter-questions of the type "Why do you ask that question?" Be prepared to explain your motives.

8 Be ready for counter-questions of the type "How do your lot do this, how is this managed in your company?"

9 Reserve time immediately after the meeting to follow up, document and discuss the information and data that emerged from the meeting. What questions still remain unanswered? What supplementary information do we need?

Interviewing Techniques

It may seem a simple matter to put questions to another person, listen to the answers and write them down. But conducting successful interviews is an art that requires both learning and practice. What we do and say and how we behave during an interview can help to make or break it, even with the best of intentions. Respondents often react more strongly to the interviewer's performance than to the actual questions he asks, so it is important for the interviewer to put his questions in a logically correct order, to listen empathetically, be responsive, and generally to act in a way that wins trust.

The first objective in an interview is to establish a cordial, professional relationship with the interviewee. There are three techniques you can use to encourage the respondent's receptivity to your questions.

Firstly, the respondent must be made to feel that he or she is getting something—new knowledge or satisfaction—out of the interview. Secondly, he or she must have a feeling that the benchmarking study will lead to something important and interesting. Thirdly, he or she must get the impression of being interviewed by a competent, professional and well-prepared person. If you bear these points in mind and do your homework well enough to satisfy the interviewee, you will considerably improve your chances of conducting an effective, result-oriented interview.

If you sense that the interview is losing momentum or that the interviewee is losing interest, there are a few effective "tricks" that you can pull out of your sleeve to get it going again. The main thing is to convey the impression that you are a good and receptive listener and that you are taking in what the interviewee is saying.

1 Register understanding and interest, for example by interjecting phrases like "I see", "You're right" or "Interesting that you should say that". This indicates to the interviewee that you are really listening and interested in what he is saying.
2 Another way to get the interviewee to tell you more is to say nothing for a moment and look at him expectantly. This gambit must be used with caution; some respondents have no more to say, and the pause may drag on into an embarrassing silence.
3 Repeat the question. This one is specially useful if the respondent does not appear to have understood the question the first time or wanders off the subject.
4 Repeat back what the respondent has just said. You can do this while writing down the answer, to emphasize the importance of the question.
5 Inject a neutral question or comment such as "I don't quite follow you, could you elaborate on that a little?" or "That sounds interesting, what exactly do you mean?"
6 Always conclude the interview by asking: "Is there anything else of interest that you think might be relevant besides what we've been talking about?"

The literature contains numerous books on interviewing technique and how to train yourself to be a good interviewer. You are advised to consult this literature if you feel uncertain or wish to improve your technique. It is not our intention to overdramatize the difficulties of interviewing, but rather to point out the great potential for success that lies in being able to establish a good, result-oriented relationship with your benchmarking partner.

Verify the Information

Make a habit of always checking out the information you have gathered. Check back with the interviewee with reference both to measurable variables and to explanatory background information.

You need not necessarily do this immediately after concluding the interview; it can wait until you need to make a fair copy or document your findings in writing. The purpose of this check is twofold:

- quality control of information received;
- verification to assure subsequent acceptance of the results of the study.

It is of course possible that errors and misunderstandings may creep into interviews and other collected information, and will need to be corrected. Failure to check the quality of data received from informants may mean that errors escape detection and, in the worst case, distort the results of the study. The need to make subsequent corrections is more the rule than the exception.

The second purpose of the checkback is to buttress the credibility of the analysis which, at a later stage, may prompt changes in your organization. Even where a subsequent check on the quality of data reveals that nothing needs to be corrected, the check is valuable in itself in that it clearly demonstrates your determination to get the facts right. However right and justified a benchmarking study may be, there is always the risk that it may be received with scepticism if the organization gets the impression that nobody has bothered to check and double-check the information.

Benchmarking Information from Other Sources

However successful you are in identifying outstanding benchmarking partners and gathering and pooling information, you may sometimes need to round out the picture to get a full appreciation of both your own business and the Best Demonstrated Practice among benchmarking partners. It may be a matter of general industrial intelligence and statistics that you can get from documents such as official reports, but also of information about specific businesses obtained for example by interviews with suppliers, customers or other users.

In the previous chapter, on Stage 2 of the benchmarking process, we listed a number of sources of information that could be helpful in identifying Best Demonstrated Practice companies. That list offers a large number of channels for seeking specific information, and for improving and increasing your knowledge of the supremacy you are looking for. Questions and uncertainties may arise in the course of the work which make it desirable to do some further checking, preferably with independent sources.

The second route, that of seeking supplementary information from customers, suppliers, and so on of the outstanding companies you have chosen as benchmarking partners, is rather more sensitive. Although we live in an open society and are at complete liberty to talk to whoever we wish, you run a serious risk of upsetting your benchmarking partners if you start interviewing their customers and suppliers without telling them about it. So if you feel the need to know more, for example about your respective customers' views on your ability to deliver value, we strongly recommend that you conduct your poll quite openly and in collaboration with your benchmarking partner. On the other hand, the facts and knowledge which can be derived from an analysis of customer-perceived value may be highly useful and valuable information that can add dimensions of depth and renewal to the benchmarking study. As a result of the explosive development of data processing technology, there are now highly sophisticated measuring instruments and analytical methods which, properly used, can be of tremendous value.

Business Ethics in Information Gathering

One of the basic principles of benchmarking is that it should take the form of an open comparison. This means that there should be no ulterior motives or other attempts to pull a fast one on your benchmarking partner. It is utterly wrong to compare benchmarking with competition analysis, or worse still with industrial espionage. Benchmarking is based on a frank and open exchange of information, in which the initiators of a benchmarking project must always be prepared to disclose the same kind of information about their own organization that they are asking their benchmarking partners to disclose about theirs.

In many studies the initiating organization opts to compare itself with more than one other, and establishes bilateral benchmarking relations in several directions. The relations established with each individual benchmarking partner are based on mutual trust and ethical use of benchmarking data. As the project manager and commissioner of a benchmarking project, you may thus have access to large quantities of information which must be treated in strictest confidence and on the highest ethical level. Even if you, as the initiator of a benchmarking project, gain access to external data from a number of world-class companies, this does not mean that you can share that information freely among them unless all have expressly agreed to permit this. Often, however, access to information and the agreement of a benchmarking partner to participate in a study are based not only on a mutual interest in pooling information about best practices, but also on guarantees of confidentiality.

It may therefore be wise to make an agreement in writing on your proposed benchmarking collaboration, with a confidentiality clause, before you actually start to gather information. Such a clause should be so written as to guarantee as far as possible that no information will be divulged without the consent of all the parties to the agreement. To minimize the risk of leaks, all information ought to be rendered anonymous. The points listed below are intended as a guide to construction of a fruitful, long-term benchmarking partnership which satisfies the highest ethical standards:

1 Document all agreements and make sure that they are understood and accepted by both parties.
2 Treat *all* information as confidential. This also includes the name of the company or organization which is your benchmarking partner. Even information which may appear trivial at first sight must nevertheless be treated as confidential. Nothing must be divulged without the express consent of your benchmarking partner.
3 The golden rule of benchmarking is that you must never ask for information or data that you would not be prepared to release yourself. This is a universal rule, and often a condition for a benchmarking partner's agreement to participate in the project.
4 Be specially meticulous when you are benchmarking a competitor. In such cases, avoid benchmarking sensitive areas such as sales or customer-oriented operations, quotation and price strategies.

5 If you collect supplementary benchmarking information by interviewing your partner's customers and suppliers, for example, you must tell them why you are doing so.

6 Sometimes a benchmarking partner makes it a condition that he wishes to remain anonymous to everybody except the project team. This condition must be respected. It is not the company as such that you are benchmarking, but its performance, and therefore the question of what is done is more important than the question of who does it.

7 Do not take advantage of information received for any other purpose than that of the benchmarking study. Thus you should not attempt to hire employees away from your partner or otherwise abuse his confidence.

There are of course a number of special cases which may not be completely covered by any of the above points, but the basic platform of benchmarking business ethics must be built on frankness, honesty, long-term mutual benefit, and businessmanship.

When is the Information Gathering Stage Over?

There is a risk of getting so caught up in the task of gathering information that you tend to keep on digging ever deeper and never stop. The answers and information you get in response to your questions prompt further questions and a desire to accumulate still more knowledge.

Except where you have unearthed some startling new element of knowledge that sheds a new light upon the whole analysis, we strongly recommend sticking to the original information-gathering plan. If you should need to supplement or clarify the data you have collected, there is always time for that during the following analytical phase. The borderline between information gathering and analysis may at times be a little fuzzy. If data gathering for some parts of the analysis looks like taking longer than expected, it is better to start the analysis with what you have than to hold up the project and disrupt the timetable by waiting until all the information is in.

7
Stage 4: Analyze

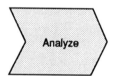

Figure 42

When you have finished gathering information, you will have large quantities of raw data. Records of interviews, replies to letters and lists of various kinds give you a body of information which must now be sorted to provide the input for a competent benchmarking analysis of your operations.

At first sight the mass of information may seem unstructured and impenetrable; the object of the fourth stage of benchmarking, analysis, is to bring order out of chaos. This fourth stage involves systematic sorting and organization of information and comparison of various measurement data with a view to identifying gaps in performance between operations and understanding the underlying operative contents and work processes which give insight into how the Best Demonstrated Practice companies achieve their excellent performance.

To enhance comparability between benchmarking companies you should also check whether there are any non-comparable factors that must be allowed for. Non-comparable factors refer to differences in operative content which are of such a kind and nature that they might risk distorting the analysis if left unadjusted. In short, you should verify that the benchmarking comparisons you make refer not only to the same fruit basket, but also to the same species of fruit.

The analytical phase also comprises documentation of the analytical results of the benchmarking study in a benchmarking report. This report is the document which contains the fact base on which rests the actual purpose of the study: to improve the performance of operations until they attain the level of excellence that you have identified as Best Demonstrated Practice. As a result of the study, some parts of your operations may turn out to be doubtful; the question may arise of whether the company should continue with certain types of internal production at all, or whether the corresponding items should be bought from outside sources instead. To answer these questions, the operations concerned should be subjected to a make-or-buy analysis.

The fourth, analytical stage of the benchmarking process thus comprises the following steps:

- Sorting and organization of information and data.
- Quality control of information.
- Correction for non-comparable factors, if any.
- Identification of performance gap to Best Demonstrated Practice and understanding of the underlying operative content that explains the existence of the gap.
- Considering a make-or-buy analysis of dubious parts of the business.

Sorting and Organizing Information

If you have followed our advice and put all documentation and processing of information into the hands of a project secretary, he or she should have all the material collected in one place. The material that has been collected should be in some sort of basic order. Use the levels of resolution and main headings that define the focus of benchmarking as a structure for the job of sorting. If for example you have decided to run a benchmarking study

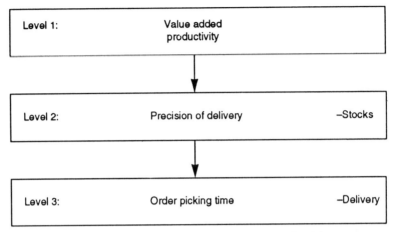

Figure 43   *If the volume of information is extensive, you should use a structure like that of the benchmarking analysis for purposes of sorting*

on three levels as shown in Figure 43, where the example refers to the purchasing function of a wholesale company, then the data should be compiled accordingly.

Comparative measurements and hard figures should be sorted in the first instance, with the collected explanatory material as a background. Use simple matrices to summarize measurements. Figure 44 shows how recorded measurements can be arranged and compared in a simple table. Here the vertical columns represent the measurements that have been selected for purposes of

	Rejects	Back orders	Precision of delivery
Own company	4.5%	3.4%	93%
Mail order business	4.2%	2.9%	95%
Electronics wholesaler	2.8%	3.0%	95%
Automotive parts supplier	3.0%	3.4%	97%

Figure 44   *Sorting data in a matrix gives a good overview*

comparison, and the horizontal lines the companies covered by the study.

The data matrices you compile are a summary of the combined efforts of the benchmarking team. You should also organize all the information and knowledge that you have documented about the various operations and levels of performance to which the information matrices belong. This whole process of sorting information can of course be greatly facilitated if it is integrated with the third-stage process of gathering information. Continuous compilation throughout the project will make the job much simpler.

Quality Control of Information

Once you have your comparative figures set up side by side in matrices according to the model proposed above, you should go through the material to check and investigate whether there are any obvious anomalies or discrepancies—whether there are figures and measurements which deviate so markedly that they can hardly be correct, or otherwise give rise to suspicions concerning the quality of the material.

There are several possible reasons why the information may fail to reflect truly the reality it is intended to measure. The benchmarking team may have misinterpreted the answers and particulars given to them in interviews and questionnaires. Or there may simply have been errors in note-taking and copying. A third possibility is that the answers and information received were simply wrong. In the previous information-gathering stage we recommended checking back with interviewees and other informants to enhance the quality of the basic data. If, despite this, you should still find obvious or suspected errors in the material, you can proceed according to the following sequence:

- Check your own material for copying or other errors that may have been made by the benchmarking team.
- Check back with the informant.
- Check other sources of information.
- Disregard the suspect information.

The time and effort you need to put into quality control of your data will naturally vary a great deal according to the complexity and focus of the benchmarking study. Although trends and tendencies can be discerned fairly easily from a report based on relatively general and superficial information, the quality of parameters and measurements of performance is still important, as we said, not just to ensure the precision of the comparisons but also to secure your organization's acceptance of the results of the benchmarking study.

When you have progressed thus far, you will have a structured set of comparative measurements and descriptions of the performance of the units you are studying, hopefully of good quality. The next important step is a thorough review and analysis to determine whether you need to make corrections for non-comparable factors.

Non-Comparable Factors

A comment which we very often hear when explaining the principles of benchmarking to various people is: "Our business is so special that I don't think you can compare us with anybody else, not even our most immediate competitor"—or words to that effect. This attitude is understandable, but still wrong. The person in charge of a business or function naturally tends to regard his or her bailiwick as unique to some extent. The daily round of toil, and the intimate knowledge of the organization's strengths and weaknesses that comes with experience, make it easy to fall into this trap. Reality, however, points in a different direction. When you start to analyze operations whose circumstances at first sight appear very different, you often find that argument after argument for the uniqueness of each falls to the ground. All organized activity follows a fundamental logic which, in a benchmarking context, can be of great value in building logical bridges and finding points of comparison.

We are not trying to assert that we live in a world of uniform organizations which can be compared with each other in all respects without distortion or fallacy. This is far from true. There is a very important step in the benchmarking process which involves identifying, analyzing and making corrections for non-comparable factors. An analysis, be it never so sophisticated, can fall flat on its face if it fails to pay sufficient heed to comparability. Non-comparable factors are circumstances and influences which tend to make a comparison "unfair"— differences which the managers of the operations concerned cannot be expected to influence within a reasonable time-frame. Identifying and making allowance for non-comparable factors is an intellectually demanding task on which a considerable amount of time must be spent. One of the chief arguments for this is that you command much greater credibility and improve the chances of your benchmarking data being accepted by your organization if you can prove that you have taken non-comparable factors into account.

The class of non-comparable factors can be divided into a number of subclasses according to the actual situation you are studying. Some typical cases, with brief examples, are cited below.

Differences in Operative Content

The first difference that springs to mind is that between the operative contents of the businesses you are comparing. There are operations in the business which differ so much in kind that performance, which is determined by operative content, cannot be compared. We can imagine a situation in which a stereo and television wholesale company wants to benchmark its delivery-from-stock function against a textile mail-order company (Figure 45). The benchmarking study is focussed on average delivery time from receipt to dispatch of orders, precision of delivery, and so on. Within this spectrum it is hoped to latch on to the excellent routines and work organization developed by the textile company. And indeed, the benchmarking team duly notes that the latter's average retrieval time per article is far shorter than the stereo and TV wholesaler's: TV sets take four times longer than garments to find in the warehouse.

Detailed investigation and analysis revealed two reasons for this:

1 The textile company used a very advanced order-picking system which enabled it to co-ordinate and utilize man-hours optimally.

2 The excellence of the system was however based on the fact that each warehouse cart could be loaded with an average of 25 orders per trip; this was naturally not possible with stereo equipment and TV sets.

Here, then, it was necessary to try to assess what the textile company's performance would be if it had to retrieve larger and heavier objects such as TV sets from its warehouse. It was found that even if the average number of orders per trip was reduced to ten (a realistic figure for handling stereo equipment and TV sets), the textile firm's average retrieval time still worked out two and a half times shorter.

Differences in Scope of Operations

If you have not previously corrected for differences in the scope of operations, you should check this point now. The term scope refers here to the degree of integration in the business.

If for example we compare an internal delivery function providing service and maintenance of buildings in a large group

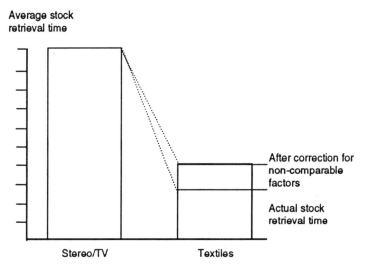

Figure 45 *The chart shows stock retrieval times for two wholesale companies, one in textiles and the other in TV and stereo equipment. Even after correction for differences in operative content (different products), the textile company works two and a half times faster*

of companies with an external supplier of the same services, their circumstances may be so different that the following effect occurs.

Operations comprise installation and trouble-shooting of plumbing and electronic systems, and are virtually identical for both organizations. A comparison of average charges showed that the outside company's prices were 3 per cent lower than the in-house department's, even though the operative content of what they did was almost identical. A more careful comparison, however, revealed that the internal department drew material from the group's material depot and its internal charges were only for labour, without materials. The external company billed materials separately, but in fact derived most of its margin contribution from material sales, so on a competitive market it quoted for labour at below cost and could still make a profit on the job as a whole. To make a fair comparison here, it was necessary to correct for the outside firm's larger scope of operations by eliminating material sales.

Differences in Market Conditions

A large retail food chain ran an internal benchmarking project to compare both customer-perceived quality and productivity, and found a wide spread of results among the shops covered by the study (Figure 46). The deviations were so great that the project team began to wonder whether there might be some additional factor that had influenced the results. To gain deeper understanding of the underlying business content, they conducted a supplementary telephone interview with a number of branch managers and asked for their comments on the results. It turned out that there was a strong correlation between the productivities of individual shops and the number of households they served. To correct for this, the team divided the shops into three groups according to their local market conditions.

Differences in Cost Position

Especially in comparisons of productivity, we often find differences in cost position which are attributable to various

Size of market

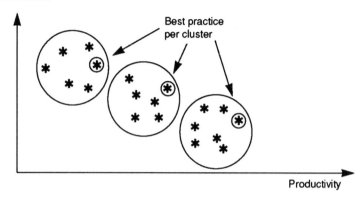

Figure 46 Simplified representation of the correlation between size of market and productivity in a retail food chain. To make the comparison fairer, outlets have been divided into three groups according to the number of households in the market served. It would be unfair to demand the same level of productivity from a rural store as from one in a residential suburb

external factors. Rentals and property prices, for example, are variables which cannot be directly influenced in the short term, even though they are negotiable and changeable in the long term. The differences are not necessarily determined in the first instance by the market; taxes and subsidies, for example, may vary from one region to another.

Some caution is needed in correcting for differences in cost position, for the causal factors may exert both positive and negative influences; a company located in a rural area, for example, may have lower personnel costs than one in a metropolitan area, but also a much lower rate of personnel turnover.

National Differences

One of the main aims of the European Community is to promote free trade so that comparative advantages and synergy effects among its member states can be utilized to the full. There will however still be differences in conditions from one EC country to another, and in some cases these may make it necessary to correct for factors which are beyond the power of the companies involved in the benchmarking study to influence. If you are making a benchmarking comparison between companies in different countries, you must be careful to find out what the situation in each country is. There may be differences in anything from environmental legislation to levels of employers' social security contributions. Demographic conditions, too, may have to be allowed for. Thus it would hardly be fair to compare the postal services in, say, Sweden and The Netherlands without taking geographic area and density of population into account.

Identifying the Performance Gap to Best Demonstrated Practice

The present chapter on the fourth stage of the benchmarking process, analysis, has dealt almost exclusively up to this point with numerical values and measures of performance. Now it is time to take the central and most important step of the analytical phase, that of studying the gap revealed by the comparative measurements in order to identify and understand the underlying performance factors which explain the origins and existence of the gap. One of the most important parts of benchmarking is of course to go on from there and draw correct and relevant conclusions from the analysis—conclusions which will serve as the essential fact input for applying the force of change that will improve results in the whole organization.

The Performance Gap

Identifying and quantifying the performance gap to your benchmarking partners is only "half" the analysis. What makes benchmarking such a powerful instrument for improvement is that it also requires you to identify and understand the underlying operative content and work processes that explain why the performance gap has arisen. The appearance of the performance gap is naturally determined by which types of performance have been benchmarked and which units have been used to measure them. As we have explained in earlier chapters, a performance gap may be represented by variables of quality or productivity, and may be expressed by a variety of measurements.

A gap is not necessarily negative (your benchmarking partner's performance is better than yours). It can also be neutral (no identifiable difference in performance between compared operations), or positive (your performance is better than your partner's).

Quantify the Gap

You can tabulate or otherwise arrange the measurements from the comparison, carefully quality-controlled and purged of non-comparable factors, to identify the performance gap between the operations which have been compared. Further on in this chapter we describe a number of highly serviceable graphic aids—such as graphs and charts—which can be used for the purpose. This book also contains a large number of figures and illustrations which exemplify performance gaps between benchmarked operations.

Underlying Operative Content

Use the knowledge and facts which have emerged from interviews and information-gathering to analyze and understand why performance differs from one organization to another. What is it in the operative content of processes and routines which explains the excellent performance achieved by your benchmarking partners? As we said before, one of the most essential steps in benchmarking involves devoting a great deal of energy to getting right to the bottom of things in order to understand why performance differs. It is this knowledge which you can apply to your own operations.

Identifying and understanding the performance gap requires detailed study and review of all the knowledge and experience that the team has accumulated as a result of the benchmarking study. The fact base, analysis and conclusions must now be documented in a Benchmarking Report.

The Benchmarking Report

To document a benchmarking study you should draw up a report describing the salient features of both fact base and conclusions. A benchmarking report should serve as:

1 A fact base for subsequent implementation of change.
2 A report for submission to the commissioner of the study.
3 Documentation of analysis as a base for future updating.
4 Experience available for future benchmarking projects in the organization.
5 Information for benchmarking partners.
6 Information for other interested parties (management, unions, etc.).

The literature contains innumerable handbooks on the art of writing reports. Benchmarking as such cannot be generalized into a simple truth, and we will not attempt here to give any general instructions on how to compose a benchmarking report. We shall content ourselves with a few short words of general advice:

- Start the report with a summary, which should give the reader a simple, precise description of the contents and give him enough information to decide whether he should read the whole report.
- Use graphs and diagrams rather than tables of figures. A graphic presentation makes a much clearer impression, and is also easier to remember.
- Supplement the graphic presentation with descriptive and explanatory comments which help the reader to understand the underlying operative content.
- A report should as far as possible be self-explanatory. It should not need an oral presentation to be understood.

One of the most important components of benchmarking is the knowledge accumulated by the benchmarking team in the course of the project. Complete success in the final implementation phase requires the fullest possible participation of the benchmarking team in that phase—both to assure the precision of the fact base that has been compiled and to supply the enthusiasm and empathy needed to help and support the rest of the organization.

Graphic Presentation

In an international perspective, there is considerable variation in the amount of importance that different people and cultures attach to matters of form. North American corporate cultures sometimes place too much faith in form; they tend to be more readily convinced by elegant charts and tables with an excellent layout than by the actual measurements and performance data which the material contains. If you show a North American company a sloppily drawn (though perfectly correct) graph or diagram, you run a grave risk of not getting the message across at all.

The Scandinavian tradition in this respect is less concerned with outward appearances; even so, it is an indisputable fact that a clear, instructive graphic presentation has high attention-getting value and is also a powerful aid to the understanding of data and their relationships. Pictures of statistical data may however vary a great deal quality-wise. Sometimes the graphs may be so complicated that the impression they give is simply confusing. Well-drawn graphs, on the other hand, especially if supported by other explanatory material, can be a very effective means of capturing interest and communicating the information that is being presented. In addition, graphic presentation often makes the data and the message easier to remember.

The type of graph or diagram you use depends on the nature of the data. Statistical science has developed a wide variety of clear, instructive and useful types of graphic presentation. In this book we have chosen a few of them as illustrative examples. The reader who wishes to learn more about this subject will find plenty of material in the literature.

The following points are important to bear in mind when you are drawing a diagram:

- Do not try to describe several phenomena in the same diagram; this is apt to be confusing.
- Every diagram should be provided with a heading and, where appropriate, a reference to the source. If you have to include

several variables in the same diagram, clarify by putting in callouts (identifying words) in the diagram itself or adding an explanatory caption.

● Make diagrams large and clear; clarify further by using scales and shading.

Cumulative Bar Charts

Cumulative bar charts are an excellent tool for describing the cost components of a value chain, for example. They are constructed of a number of bars forming a stepped curve. The one reproduced in Figure 47 shows how the cost mass is built up in the value chain that leads from the production of a loaf of bread through distribution to sale to the consumer.

Graphs with a Time Axis

To understand the underlying performance that explains the excellence of a Best Demonstrated Practice company, it is often necessary to analyze its operations over a period of years. This puts development into a historical perspective, which can be

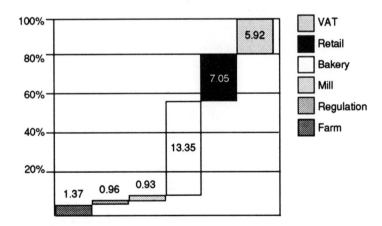

Figure 47 *Cumulative bar charts are admirably suited to illustrating the buildup of costs in a value chain*

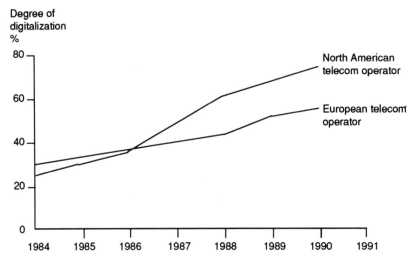

Degree of digitalization %

Figure 48   *Digitalization strongly influences both quality and productivity. The faster rate of progress in North America will substantially upgrade the operator's productivity, mainly in the areas of remote monitoring and trouble-shooting*

succinctly described by a graph with a time axis. Figure 48 illustrates the growth of digitalization in European and North American telecom networks.

This graph clearly shows that the North American operator is digitalizing its operations at a faster pace than its European counterpart. Since the degree of digitalization is an important productivity factor in the telecommunications industry, the graph serves its purpose by contributing elements of knowledge that help to explain differences and similarities in productivity between national telecom operators.

Bar Charts

Bar charts offer an admirable means of illustrating both functions as a whole and their component subfunctions. The one in Figure 49 represents total cost per invoice broken down into cost components.

Properly used, the bar chart communicates a quick and simple picture of both the whole and the component parts. It can be used to express both absolute figures and percentages.

Cost per invoice

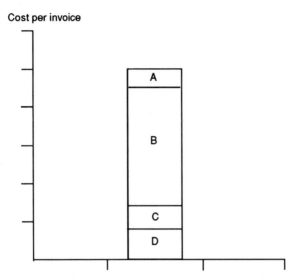

Figure 49 *Bar charts provide clear, easy-to-grasp information*

Figure 50 shows how the bar chart model can be used to illustrate successively finer levels of resolution. The first level of resolution, cost per invoice, is the same as in the previous figure. At the next level, the personnel cost element is broken down into its components, while the third level analyzes the relationship between fixed and variable wage costs.

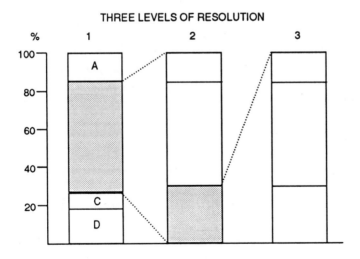

Figure 50 *A bar chart can be broken down into several levels*

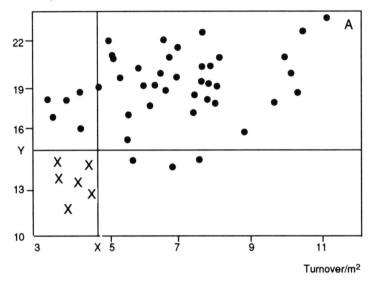

Figure 51   *This graph shows margin contribution as a function of turnover per unit of sales area in a retail chain. The shops in the bottom left corner are "basket cases"*

Graphic Illustration of Correlations

You frequently find relationships between variables in your material which you want to illustrate graphically. You may have identified more than one criterion for measurement of a given performance which you wish to analyze conjointly. Figure 51 illustrates the relationship between turnover per unit of floor area and margin contribution in a chain of food retail shops analyzed in an internal benchmarking study. The two lines that divide the graph represent profitability cutoff points:

1 No branch with a turnover per square metre to the left of line X is profitable.
2 No branch with a margin contribution below line Y is profitable.

The branch marked *A* is the one with the Best Demonstrated Practice according to these criteria. The branches grouped in the bottom left rectangle are "basket cases"—hopelessly unprofitable.

Their margin contributions and sales per square metre are lower than those of any profitable branch in the chain.

As we have said, the number of variants that can be used to describe relationships and contribute to understanding and identification of Best Demonstrated Practice and its underlying operative content is very large—almost infinite. There are of course no universal rules stating which model or type of diagram is best for illustrating them; the choice depends very much on the situation.

Make-or-Buy Analysis

There is a decision point that comes before you proceed to the implementation phase. First you ought to consider the question of whether the operation you have studied should be continued at all as an in-house activity, or whether there are grounds for buying the same services on the open market instead. This decision is made on the basis of the knowledge that the benchmarking study has provided about the performance of your own business compared to that of others in the outside world (Figure 52). To decide whether an operation is best performed by your own organization or somebody else, you can subject it to a make-or-buy analysis. Candidates for such an analysis are operations which are peripheral to the core business of the organization, such as staff functions or internal contracting units.

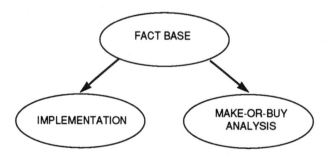

Figure 52   *The benchmarking analysis supplies a fact base which may raise the question of whether certain parts of the business should be kept on or farmed out. In such cases a make-or-buy analysis is advised*

Analysis of which activities the organization should handle itself, and which it should buy from outside, aims at sharpening the focus on core business and increasing the productivity of the organization. A make-or-buy analysis starts by determining whether the contribution which a function makes to value creation in the business is greater than the cost of producing that contribution. If so, you should either go on manufacturing the product (or providing the service) or set up your own production facilities. If however the cost exceeds the contribution to creation of value, the function should be discontinued and its contribution should be bought instead.

A make-or-buy analysis is actually based on three considerations: macroeconomics, degree of integration, and developments over a period of time.

1 Market economy has proved to be more efficient than planned economy. This is because buyers in the former can choose between alternatives, which they cannot do in the latter. The alternative which is not chosen must either go out of business or strive to perform better. Where a product or service is supplied within an organization in which the buyer or user has no choice of other suppliers, the same major drawback applies as in a planned economy: there is simply no spur to supply it efficiently.

2 The second point is the matter of vertical integration. Many organizations devote a large share of their efforts to activities which only support the activities which are their actual corporate mission. In many cases they make things for themselves which they could buy cheaper from somebody else. In addition, the resources of management are divided, and focus on the core business is easily lost. The classic case is that of Henry Ford, who owned forests and mines to produce wood and steel as raw materials for his automobiles.

3 An additional point, of course, is that products which once made a significant contribution to the core business have grown trivial with time and can now be bought more cheaply than they can be made. This implies that make-or-buy analyses ought to be repeated from time to time to ensure that the focus remains on core business.

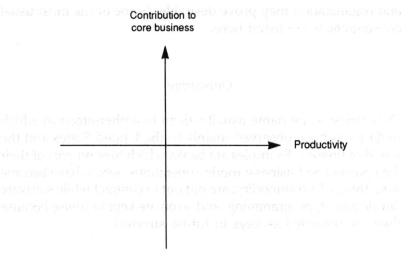

Figure 53 *The graph illustrates the relationship between relative contributions to core business and productivity. If an operation does not substantially contribute to the core business its continued existence should be questioned, especially if its productivity is low*

Figure 53 illustrates a key issue of make-or-buy analysis, that of whether a given operation contributes to the company's core business and whether it is performed with high productivity. Operations located in the lower left quadrant, i.e. those whose productivity and contribution to core business are both low, should be discontinued. Operations which are highly productive but which contribute relatively little to core business (lower right quadrant) ought to be hived off as separate companies, and possibly sold. Operations in the upper left quadrant, which contribute significantly to core business but with low productivity, must be subjected to strong pressure to rationalize so that they do not injure the company's competitive position by increasing its costs. Operations in the upper right quadrant, with high productivity and a relatively high contribution, should of course be retained and developed.

Consequences of a Make-or-Buy Analysis

The make-or-buy analysis may naturally result in various consequences to the operation concerned. Changes in both scope and organization may prove desirable. Some of the most usual consequences are listed here.

Outscoring

Outscoring is the name usually given to a phenomenon which to date has been observed mainly in the United States and the world of finance. Examples are banks which hive off part of their data processing business; routine operations, which have become something of a commodity, are put out to contract while software development, programming, and so on are kept in-house because they are regarded as keys to future survival.

Companization

The question of companization (shorthand for breaking a function out of an organization and making a separate company of it) arises if the function or operation concerned produces only commodity-type goods or services, but does so with great efficiency. One example of this is SAS Service Partner. As the in-flight catering function of Scandinavian Airline Systems it was highly productive, but what it produced was neither unique nor an essential part of the airline's core business. Since becoming a company in its own right, divorced from SAS's core business, it has been highly successful.

Privatization

A gradual change of values has taken place in public administration. In the countries of Western Europe it is no longer considered essential for the public sector to be the producer of the services it is committed to providing. In other words the provision of, say, pre-primary schools is not regarded as a significant value-generating contribution to the core business of local authorities. The conclusion, consequently, is that all or part of that service should be privatized.

Selling Off

Functions or parts of businesses whose productivity and contribution to core business are low should be sold off. This includes support functions like the printing shops, research departments and preventive health care departments with which large corporations and administrations have encumbered themselves.

Integration

The result of a make-or-buy analysis may of course also be a decision to *start* manufacturing a product instead of buying it as hitherto. A good example of this is the Swedish-based IKEA furniture chain. Previously, IKEA did not manufacture its own furniture because this was not felt to contribute enough to the basic corporate mission, which was to sell furniture at the lowest possible price. Today, with a collapsing manufacturing industry in Eastern Europe, the situation has changed; IKEA has had to revise its policy and been abruptly compelled to start manufacturing furniture in order to meet the commitments of its core business.

Decision Parameters in a Make-or-Buy Analysis

There are several important questions to be considered in connection with a make-or-buy analysis. Some of the parameters which affect the decision are quantifiable, others are matters of judgement. However, the precision of decision-making can be improved if the right questions are asked and answered, even if the answers cannot always be quantified.

Here follow some of the parameters which are crucial to a decision whether to make something or buy it from outside sources.

Productivity

The productivity aspect means comparing the cost per unit produced to the cost of buying from other suppliers. If productivity is low, in-house production should be discontinued and the product or service should be bought instead.

Customer-Perceived Value

Here the question is whether or not a given activity represents added value from the customer's point of view. Are the company's products or services more attractive to customers because it handles the activity in question itself?

Availability

If the product or service is hard to obtain from other sources, this strengthens the case for in-house production. But if it is freely available on the open market, buying should be considered.

Focus on Core Business

Activities which cannot be classed under the heading of core business tend to distract the attention of management from its core business. Experience suggests that this consideration has greater weight in times of adversity, whereas the need for concentration is not so keenly felt in times of prosperity.

Fixed Costs

Absorption of fixed costs is a tricky aspect. If an activity carries an allocated share of joint costs, those costs will have to be borne by the rest of the business if it is dropped.

Conversion Costs

All the time and expense involved in switching from internal to external supply must also be taken into account. This question can suitably be dealt with in the form of an investment calculation.

In a make-or-buy analysis, just as in benchmarking, it is important to take great pains to research and verify the fact base. A make-or-buy analysis can have far-reaching consequences for the business as a whole. At present there is a strong tendency in both business and administration to concentrate activities on basic skills and to put support functions on a market-economy footing to a greater degree than before, i.e. to buy products and services from outside rather than produce them internally.

In the fourth, analytical, stage of the benchmarking process we have organized, quality-controlled and analyzed the voluminous information material collected in the previous stage. The analysis has identified and cast light upon the performance, i.e. the operative content and processes, which explains the excellence of the organizations with the Best Demonstrated Practice, in such a way that understanding has been attained. A benchmarking report has been written containing an account of the fact base that has been compiled, including explanatory analyses. To be somewhat provocative, we could say that we have now reached the point where the *real* work starts: the work of making changes, based on the new knowledge acquired from benchmarking partners, with a view to making the business more efficient.

In the next chapter we shall discuss an approach to leading the organization from knowledge of what can be achieved to actual achievement.

8
Stage 5: Implement for Effect

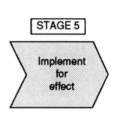

Figure 54

The fifth stage of the benchmarking process comprises the work of closing the gap which the analytical stage has identified, and translating the potential for improvement into tangible results. Measures must now be taken to realize the potential that has been identified within the line organization. Does the identified benchmarking result fit in with the regular business plan, or will recalibration be needed? The results of the benchmarking study must be formulated as new goals for the business. These goals must then be broken down according to the chosen model, either in a process approach or in the regular line organization. When this has been done, you must draw up a plan for implementation including specific plans for each part of the organization that will be affected.

The fifth stage of benchmarking, implementation for effect, thus comprises the following steps:

- Consider the implications of the results.
- Integrate with the regular business plan.

- Prepare a plan for changes to be made.
- Implement the plan.

Consider the Implications of the Results

The analytical phase identified the gap to benchmarking partners. Depending on the content and structure of the project, the gap may refer to various areas. If the benchmarking study has focussed on customer-perceived value, there will probably be a larger share of "soft" explanatory factors. If on the other hand the study has concentrated on productivity and costs, it will probably yield more hard figures relating to value added, productivity per employee, throughput times, and so on.

Report the Results of the Study to the People it Affects

Before the implementation phase gets to the stage of practical application in the organization, the benchmarking study must be reported to and accepted by the key people in the organization whom it affects. The results must of course be reported to the top management or management group, but also to all the middle managers whose areas of responsibility are likely to be affected by the process of implementation. It is particularly important to secure the full concurrence of top management with the conclusions presented to them in the report. Top management should assess the report primarily with reference to its factual content. Another important criterion for assessment is whether the report appears to be neutral and impartial. The impartiality aspect is specially important if the benchmarking team has no outside representatives but is made up exclusively of people from inside the organization. Presentation to top management is a critical point; it is essential to secure their full approval of the results of the study.

Immediately thereafter the study must also be reported to people at middle management level. These people have certainly been involved to a greater or lesser degree in the information-gathering and analytical phases, so it is important that they should fully accept the study, especially with regard to its factual content and the quality of the data. If you do not succeed in getting your results agreed by the organization, the implementation phase is bound to run into obstacles when it gets under way.

Trade union representatives are a third group of interested parties to whom the study may need to be reported and presented. Benchmarking studies, by virtue of their fact-based nature, are generally well received by this group too; they give union representatives, like everybody else, an input for decision about changes based on known and confirmed facts. Especially in connection with projects where the conclusions point to problems of over-manning, we have found by experience that fact-based benchmarking is a very persuasive instrument to use in negotiations with unions.

Opportunities for Improvement

Once the results of the study have been reported to all the interested parties in the organization, it is time to start translating the conclusions into opportunities for improvement and new target figures. On the basis of the gap that the benchmarking study has revealed and the knowledge of the underlying operative content that has been gained, the opportunities for improvement should be evaluated, defined and quantified. Ways and means of making improvements should be discussed with the people affected by the results of the study. If the project has taken the form of a process study that cuts across lines of demarcation in the organization, it is important to involve all the affected parts of the organization.

The benchmarking team must play an active part at this stage. During the information-gathering and analytical stages its members have acquired a fund of detailed knowledge both of their own operations and of those of the benchmarking partners they have studied. It is now up to them to pass on this knowledge to their colleagues so that the potential for improvement indicated by the benchmarking gap can be translated as faithfully as possible into the language that the organization speaks. It is the task of the benchmarking team to draw up a plan for change based on the knowledge and input communicated to the organization by the discussions. The plan should specify the measures judged necessary to close the benchmarking gap. When this plan has been drafted, it must be checked against and integrated with the organization's regular business plan.

Integrate with the Regular Business Plan

Most companies and organizations work to a more or less detailed business plan of some kind. Implementation of action to improve results on the basis of the benchmarking project must not of course be allowed to conflict with the aims or level of ambition of the regular business plan. On the contrary, the two should be integrated so that they work in harmony or even in synergy to achieve the best possible result. Where a benchmarking study has been made of the business as a whole, its results may carry sufficient weight to justify a revision or fine-tuning modification of the entire business plan. If on the other hand the benchmarking study has been concerned with only parts or small sections of the business, its effects on the overall business plan will be of a less critical nature.

Draw up a Plan for Implementation

When the results of the study have been fully accepted by all concerned in the organization and the potential for improvement with reference to the benchmarking gap has been evaluated, it is time to formulate new goals and aims.

The goals formulated by the organization need to be carefully analyzed. The expectations which formulation of a goal implies must be based on businesslike assessments, and not an expression of pious management hopes. If goals and aims are to be practical tools for stretching the organization to its full potential, their criteria must be challenging yet realistic. Goals must be formulated in such a way as to define:

- What performance is attainable according to the benchmarking gap.
- What performance the organization is capable of achieving.

With benchmarking as the foundation this process, otherwise so complex and time-consuming, is already far advanced thanks to the points of comparison.

The task involves not only formulating overall goals, but also breaking them down into goals for each part of the organization. Goals should be broken down in a hierarchy corresponding to the structure of the organization, derived from the overall goals and proceeding on down. Just as in earlier phases it is important to secure full acceptance of the proposed measures and plans that the new goals and aims entail. When breaking down goals within the organization you should proceed from its internal customer–supplier structure; thus goals for the central accounting department should be formulated on the basis of the demands that the users of its services (in-house customers) make on it.

When drafting an implementation plan it is advisable to give thought to the sequence of actions, costs and timetable.

1 *Sequence of actions*
  The order in which measures are implemented will obviously depend on what aspects of performance are to be changed and improved. Obviously, the knowledge derived from the benchmarking project should be utilized. Here again, the benchmarking team has an active part to play. Its members should act as catalysts in the process of change. And if the benchmarking process is part of a larger process of change, the plan of action should of course be integrated with the overall plan.

2 *Costs*
  Even if the identified potential for improvement is huge and the need to do something about it is obvious, you should always make a habit of costing the process of change. It is good practice to have constant control of the usage of resources and expenditure of funds which the process involves.

3 *Timetable*
  How have you calculated the timetable for your process of change? Many companies and organizations prefer to link it to the regular budget cycle. Our opinion, based on experience, is that improvement should be a continuous process subject to a minimum of constraint from budget routines, etc. There is no point in delaying action to improve efficiency if you can start right away.

Implement the Plan

Whereas the three previous headings referred to the preparation of a plan for change, this fourth heading refers to its ultimate purpose: to proceed from thought to deed and achieve a measurable improvement in the organization's performance. Having taken part in a large number of implementation projects, we have identified some success factors which are important to remember if the purpose is to be accomplished:

1 *Full management participation*
A process of change affects all levels of management in the organization. Nobody can afford to stand on the sidelines and watch while the work is in progress. Total success depends on total participation. As far as possible, people other than department heads should also be involved in the process.
2 *Commitment*
The success of the project is conditional not only on the participation, but also on the personal commitment of all concerned. In benchmarking, commitment often comes as a bonus because the method *per se* focusses attention on performance and operative content. It stimulates the urge to perform well that is present to a greater or lesser degree in all of us. The will to excel and be more professional encourages commitment to the task.
3 *Understanding of corporate goals and strategies*
To move towards a goal in a process of change, it is necessary for the organization's goals and strategies to be communicated and explained to everybody. Delegated goals and changes are mainly of an operative nature, but it must always be possible to relate them to overall goals and strategies.
4 *Definite timetable and plan of action*
Good planning, expressed in a concrete plan of action and a definite timetable, always contributes to the success of a project. The plan of action is important in that it makes everybody aware of what the project entails, and the timetable must of course be kept to live up to the expectations of whoever commissioned the project.
5 *Management concentration on the project*
One thing that can ruin not only the process of implementation

but even the whole benchmarking project is lack of interest on the part of top management. A process of change is not something that the leadership of an organization can delegate and watch from the sidelines. Success and improvement of results demand wholehearted backing from the top.

6 *Information*

Information is a large and hazy concept. It is another of those things like love and money that you can never have enough of. When we speak of information in the present case we mean not only the duty of the project management to supply information, but also the duty of the organization to seek it. The project management should preferably maintain a set of documentation, an information base, which anybody who is interested can consult on their own initiative to learn the details of the project. In addition, the project management should issue bulletins at regular intervals.

7 *Energy and perseverance*

It cannot be repeated too often that a successful process of change demands energy and perseverance on the part of the people involved. Proceeding from ear of corn to loaf of bread by initiating, pursuing, implementing and completing a benchmarking project calls for energy and perseverance in large measure if the project is not to lose momentum.

Benchmarking: a Repetitive Process

Successful benchmarking is not a once-for-all action. Benchmarking can attain its full effect only by repetition. When you have been through the process for the first time you not only have a working model that can be used again, you also have an established interface of contacts.

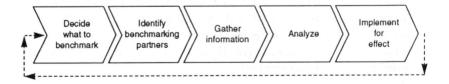

Figure 55

Earlier in this book we characterized benchmarking as a method for constant and continuous improvement. That may sound like a bold claim, but the fact is that our total experience of benchmarking as a tool for improving results is so encouraging that we repeat and maintain our claim without hesitation.

9
From Benchmarking to Benchlearning

In the introductory chapter to this book we described the force for cultural change which benchmarking, properly applied, has proved capable of exerting. It shifts the focus of attention of people and organizations from all kinds of trivialities to what is fundamental to their individual and collective success, namely the actual operative content of what they are doing. But it needs to be supported by a process of development which should run parallel to, and thus accompany, the process of benchmarking.

Benchmarking is actually a matter of imitating successful behaviour. This is exactly what Peter Senge, E. H. Schein and others are advocating when they speak of the learning organization—codifying successful behaviour. That is what benchmarking is all about.

Leadership Development and Training

If you start a process of leadership development and training concurrently with benchmarking, the two will reinforce each other, dramatically enhancing both learning and its effects. People get more interested when what they learn is directly related to their work and skill training takes place on the job (Figure 56).

Another way to put it from the employer's point of view is that the focus shifts from the individual's principal concern,

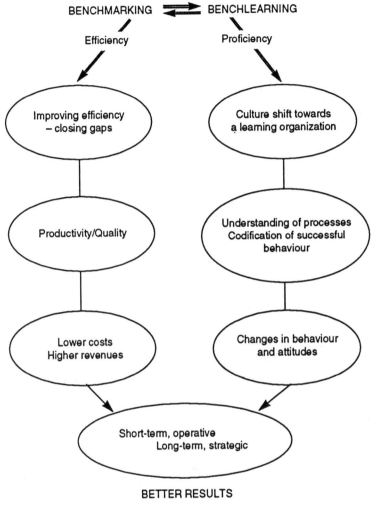

BENCHMARKING ⇄ BENCHLEARNING

Efficiency   Proficiency

Improving efficiency
– closing gaps

Culture shift towards
a learning organization

Productivity/Quality

Understanding of processes
Codification of successful
behaviour

Lower costs
Higher revenues

Changes in behaviour
and attitudes

Short-term, operative
Long-term, strategic

BETTER RESULTS

Figure 56

which is to acquire more education for his or her own benefit, to that of the employer, which is to run the business more efficiently. This is in fact one of the classic problems of personnel development and human resource management—that of finding methods of developing organizations and individuals which offer more benefit to the organizer of the schemes than to the individuals who participate in them.

As we mentioned earlier, there is considerable scepticism about the value of current types of leadership development programmes to the company which pays for them. The few studies that have been made in this area indicate the reverse, in fact: that the utility to the employer/paying customer is small compared to the utility to the trainee. This probably helps to explain why training and leadership development have come to be regarded as employee fringe benefits disguised under the cloak of utility to the organization. By this we mean that training and development are often a ritual, a kind of rain-dance, performed in the belief that it will bring success to the organization. It is like being a member of the ruling class in Baghdad; nobody dares refuse an invitation to dinner from Saddam Hussein. In the same way, no company dares drop its advanced leadership development programmes, even when they are run at a substantial loss. It is simply not done to question a company's duty to foster its executives. These programmes often survive longer than marketing budgets in times of cutbacks.

We make so bold as to claim that what we call benchlearning is a way to relate leadership development and training to the needs of business and thus make them directly beneficial to the organization. By systematically linking learning and theory to the operative content of the business, the employer can get much more mileage out of the money he spends on development and training.

We have already described the five stages of benchmarking:

1 Decide what to benchmark.
2 Identify benchmarking partners.
3 Gather information.
4 Analyze.
5 Implement for effect.

Our choice of the number of stages was made mainly on practical grounds. There are certainly many other sequences which give equally good results. We are agnostics in this respect; we do not believe that any particular model is the sole route to salvation. We have found, however, that our division of the process is practical, serviceable and easy to follow.

A process of learning can be similarly structured in conjunction with a benchmarking process. Sometimes the object of benchmarking is to make a one-off comparison for a single definitive correction of a function which is not performing adequately. Generally, however, benchmarking marks the dawning of a new cultural era characterized by curiosity, entrepreneurialism and constant learning.

The Six Stages of Benchlearning

Our advice to you, dear reader, is to couple a leadership development process and training scheme to benchmarking. The process can conveniently be divided into a number of stages, six to be precise, as follows:

1 Having the will and courage to gain insight.
2 Finding out what is known about the subject, and by whom.
3 Acquiring information and absorbing knowledge.
4 Internalizing and pooling experience to cement knowledge.
5 Codifying successful behaviour and changing the work process.
6 Training skills: applying knowledge and proficiency.

Let us briefly review each of these links in the learning chain. The aim of this process in connection with benchmarking is not to teach one lesson once for all, but *to create an environment which rewards constant learning with better performance and, in consequence, with greater success.*

Having the Will and Courage to Gain Insight

The will to change is often low in employees as a group, as well as in members of management. This applies particularly to parts of organizations whose performance is not measured by a profit-and-loss account. Sometimes they try to prove their importance to the organization by the size of their budget and the numbers on their payroll rather than by performance that contributes to the working unit and its processes. Often they see no reason to question what they are doing because nobody else questions it, and they feel it is far too dangerous to expose their operations to the mechanisms of market economy. Their performance can however be judged by comparison with similar operations elsewhere. What is needed is a catalyst in the organization to start the cultural reappraisal which is required to make heads of functional units feel successful if they make an effort to find objects of comparison in the outside world, and then make the comparisons and accept all the consequences they entail. The will and the motive force to make such comparisons must be injected by the higher executives who are responsible for the success of the organization as a whole.

Finding Out What is Known about the Subject, and by Whom

Once an organization has been persuaded to want to acquire new knowledge, and dares to prove to the world and itself that it accepts the fact that it is not the world champion, the next step is to find out where to look for new knowledge. Active seeking after knowledge is not something that can be taken for granted in modern organizations. The authors have had contacts with an insurance company whose premiums for boat insurance have been excessively high for the past ten years. They have not even been able to make their all-in customers a decent offer when it comes to insuring boats. In all these years, that company has never taken the trouble to analyze the value chain of boat insurance to find out why its premiums are not competitive. A few hypotheses in this particular case are:

1 Lack of productivity in the organization.
2 Allocation of joint costs in a way that does not reflect actual consumption of resources.
3 Differences in frequency of claims on insured items.

In the present case the conditions were identical, so there were no differences in quality to be investigated. The company has not analyzed the reasons for its lack of competitiveness. It has not even bothered to find out how other companies manage things more efficiently. This, of course, is a question of wanting and daring, but also very much a question of where the information can be found and exactly what information needs to be acquired. A benchmarking process is not necessarily the most effective answer in this case. There may very well be alternative processes for gathering relevant information from the outside world.

The important thing about benchmarking, however, is that it strips away blinkers and creates a receptiveness and openness to new information from outside sources. If the motivation is there, and if people can overcome their fear of displaying weakness—if they dare, in other words—the problem is one of where knowledge can be acquired most effectively. Acquiring information and processing it to knowledge is something that must almost always take place largely outside normal working hours. Reading specialist articles and books is a natural pastime, for example, for members of all companies which live on knowledge.

Acquiring Information and Absorbing Knowledge

Processed information is called knowledge. The conversion of information to knowledge implies that the right of interpretation passes from the sender to the receiver. What happens is quite simply that the receiver digests the mass of information and comes to an understanding of how the elements of information have been applied in various contexts to bring about change and improvement. Information is really nothing but data, whereas knowledge is data processed by an individual in such a way as to be useful to that individual.

Internalizing and Pooling Experience to Cement Knowledge

Internalizing and pooling experience mean that new insights have been subjected to an iterative process and come to be acknowledged by the individual as an acceptable or successful pattern of behaviour. The receiver's curiosity has been aroused to the point where he or she asks the next question and the one after that: Why? Why? Why? This internalization and interaction with the supplier of the knowledge prepares the individual to proceed to action. Knowledge needs, so to speak, to be refined to skill in order to be applied to the particular work process for which the receiving individual is responsible.

Codifying Successful Behaviour and Changing Work Process

Once this has happened, it is possible to codify successful behaviour, whereupon a change in the actual work process can occur. The earlier stages, so to speak, were necessary in order to prepare the receiving individual to apply his new knowledge to his own situation. Now the time has come to move on from thought to deed.

It is a characteristic feature of what are commonly called learning organizations that they are able to codify successful behaviour. However it is a question not of ability alone, but also of determination and will to act. For the process of describing, codifying and propagating successful behaviour costs money. This is a case of investing in development of skills, which is a particularly painful form of economic sacrifice. It is far, far easier for a corporate management to decide to invest in hardware such as plant or machinery than to make a similar decision about software. There is evidently a fundamental psychological distinction here: an investment in something tangible is regarded as a safe asset, whereas a leader probably never feels really certain that an investment in software is going to pay off. Investing in his own employees and executives is not necessarily going to lead to higher future profitability for the organization that does the paying; people can quit their present jobs and go to work for somebody else, in which case the second employer reaps the benefit of the investment that the first one has made in development of skills.

Training Skills: Applying Knowledge and Proficiency

Changing work processes, codifying successful behaviour, training people and developing leaders is a long-drawn-out, expensive business. The bright side to this gloomy picture is that the culture created in the process lives on as the norm, even though individuals may quit and go to other employers. Once you have succeeded in establishing a cultural pattern that centres on learning, your investment is secured, so to speak. The process of institutionalizing this cultural pattern comprises a number of elements, of which a well-planned, continuous benchmarking process is the most important.

The great and serendipitous advantage of "benchlearning" is that the cost of reorienting a cultural pattern towards learning and enhancement of proficiency is low, because the payoff actually comes while the process is going on in the form of more efficient performance.

In the longer term, codification of work processes is translated into applied knowledge, skill training and a higher level of proficiency. There is however a risk that the learning process may peter out after codification and learning have reached a new and higher level. The authors recently met some consultant colleagues whom we had been out of touch with for about eight years. We had collaborated with them then on developing certain concepts which subsequently exerted a powerful influence on the market. When we met them again and brought each other up to date, it turned out that those concepts were still the same as they had been eight years before. No further development had taken place; the codified knowledge had, so to speak, been cocooned. In the light of this story, let us emphasize that it is more important to achieve a permanent state of ongoing development than a given stage of development. The desire, not to raise the level of knowledge on one occasion but constantly to acquire new knowledge and translate it into skills, is the culture-bearing element in a learning organization.

Benchmarking presents an unlooked-for opportunity to make the dream of a learning organization come true. A number of techniques under the name of benchlearning have been developed to do this, but they will be the subject of another book.

Bibliography

Berggren, Eric. *Benchmarking—ett sätt att lära av andra*. Institutet för verkstadsteknisk forskning (1992).

Briner, Wendy, Geddes, Michael and Hastings, Colin. *Project Leadership*. Van Nostrand Reinhold, New York (1990).

Camp, Robert C. *Benchmarking. The Search for Industry Best Practices that Lead to Superior Performance*. ASQC Industry Press, Milwaukee, Wisconsin; Quality Resources, New York (1989).

Gordon, Gilbert and Pressman, Israel. *Quantitative Decision-Making for Business*, 2nd edn. Prentice-Hall International, Englewood Cliffs, NJ (1990).

Gustafsson, Lennart. *Snabbare företag genom klokare arbete*. Sveriges Mekanförbund (1991).

Jarenko, Leenamaija and Vahlgren Wall, Maria. *Information som konkurrensmedel*. IHM Läromedel, Gothenburg (1986).

Karlöf, Bengt. *Business Strategy In Practice*. Wiley, Chichester (1987).

Lindén, Lena. *Att rita diagram av statistiska data*. Studentlitteratur, Lund (1981).

Peters, Thomas J. and Waterman, Robert H. Jr. *In Search of Excellence: Lessons from America's Best Run Companies*. HarperCollins, New York (1982).

Spendolini, Michael J. *The Benchmarking Book*. Amacom (1992).

Thompson, Arthur A. Jr. and Strickland, A.J. III. *Strategic Management—Concepts and Cases*, 5th edn. Irwin, Homewood, Ill. (1990).

Index

Index compiled by Margaret Cronan